Other Books by Terry Glaspey

BOOK LOVER'S GUIDE TO
GREAT
READING

A Guided Tour of Classic
& Contemporary Literature

Terry W. Glaspey

InterVarsity Press
Downers Grove, Illinois

InterVarsity Press
P.O. Box 1400, Downers Grove, IL 60515-1426
World Wide Web: www.ivpress.com
E-mail: mail@ivpress.com

InterVarsity Press® is the book-publishing division of InterVarsity Christian Fellowship/USA®, a student
movement active on campus at hundreds of universities, colleges and schools of nursing in the United States
of America, and a member movement of the International Fellowship of Evangelical Students. For
information about local and regional activities, write Public Relations Dept., InterVarsity Christian
Fellowship/USA, 6400 Schroeder Rd., P.O. Box 7895, Madison, WI 53707-7895.

Cover photograph: Kathy Burrows

ISBN 0-8308-2329-8

Printed in the United States of America ∞

Library of Congress Cataloging-in-Publication Data

Glaspey, Terry W.
  Book lover's guide to great reading : a guided tour of classic and contemporary
literature / Terry W. Glaspey.
    p. cm.
  Includes bibliographical references.
  ISBN 0-8308-2329-8 (alk. paper)
    1. Christians—Books and reading. 2. Christians—Books and reading—Bibliography. 3.
  Christian literature—Bibliography. 4. Best books. I. Title.
Z1039.C47 G58 2001
230—dc21
                                                                              2001024041

23 22 21 20 19 18 17 16 15 14 13 12 11 10 9 8 7 6 5 4 3 2 1

21 20 19 18 17 16 15 14 13 12 11 10 09 08 07 06 05 04 03 02 01

CONTENTS

ONE

WELCOME TO THE ADVENTURE
OF READING

L et me begin with a heartfelt confession.

I admit it. I am a biblioholic, one who loves books and whose life would seem incomplete without them. I am an addict, with a compulsive need to stop by nearly any bookstore I pass in order to get my fix. Books are an essential part of my life, the place where I have spent many unforgettable moments. For me, reading is one of the most enjoyable ways to pass a rainy afternoon or a leisurely summer day. I crave the knowledge and insights that truly great books bring into my life and can spend transported hours scouring used book stores for volumes which "I simply must have." I love the smell and feel of well-loved books and the look of a bookcase full of books waiting to be taken down and read.

My love of reading came into my life at about the same time as my conversion. I had a hunger to learn more about the faith I had newly embraced, so I began to read just about everything I could get my hands on: biographies of famous Christians both past and present, books explaining and defending Christian doctrine, books on deepening the spiritual life and books that elucidated the meaning of the greatest of all books, the Bible. At that time my search for understanding and learning seemed unquenchable. To be honest, it still does.

If you picked up a copy of this book, it is probably because you share my addiction. But also like me, you may sometimes find yourself overwhelmed by all the choices offered on the shelves of the bookstore and the library. King Solomon noted that there was no end to the publishing of books, but that was before the invention of the printing press. Think what he might say about the present profusion of books! Every year publishers churn out thousands of titles to add the millions already available.

But here's the rub. The majority of books being published are generally not worth the time and effort it takes to read them. They might be derivative, poorly written, based on poor thinking and research, trashy or heretical, or might suffer from some other fault. Why waste your time with these when there are so many really good books that you've never read or maybe even heard of yet?

That's where *this* book comes in. It's purpose is this: to help you sort through the overwhelming number of options so that you can spend your reading time on the very best books. In the pages that follow, you'll find recommendations for exploring the classic books of the Christian tradition and other great classics, the best in contemporary literature, books that will help you develop a stronger intellectual basis for your faith, books that will help your spiritual life grow and flourish, and the finest in children's literature. Now, I don't claim to be an expert in every area where I'll be making recommendations. I'm just someone who has read a lot and wishes to pass on some suggestions about the books that I've enjoyed and that have made an impact on my life and thinking. Along the way, though, I have paid careful attention to the experts and consulted countless other recommended reading lists to try to make this list as helpful as possible. And while it makes no claim to include every great book, you won't find anything listed here that's not worth exploring.

These lists reflect my commitment to the Christian worldview, and the books listed here are evaluated from that perspective. I have found, though, that many of my fellow believers are not among the most avid of readers and that when they do read a book, it is often only the most shallow and experiential sort of Christian self-help volume. I hope this book might prove an inspiring guide for such readers to begin to read more widely and with greater discernment. If modern evangelicals do not tend to be great lovers of books, then they have, sadly, wandered away from a long tradition of Christians who placed great value on books and reading.

If you make it a goal in life to constantly keep your mind open to new ideas and to better understand the beliefs and values you already hold, then books become a necessary companion on the journey of life. How important are books? Well, God himself chose the medium of a book as a primary way to communicate to us the truth of his love and grace. And the exploits of the great heroes of the faith and the life of Christ himself are also forever revealed and offered to us in this same book.

* * *

In studying church history, we find that many great leaders and thinkers were set on their path of faith through the agency of a book that transformed their life or their way of thinking. Following are some examples.

The writings of Augustine were a great help to a young monk named Martin Luther, who was struggling with the weight of his sin and his inability to gain the confidence that God had forgiven him. Augustine enlightened Luther's study of the book of Romans and opened him up to a new understanding of the meaning of grace, faith and salvation. Augustine's books helped Martin Luther to clarify and solidify his understanding of justification by faith alone. In turn, Luther used pamphlets and books to spread the message of the Reformation.

The origins of the Pietist movement, which brought about much-needed revival to the church, were not linked to a mass movement, a memorable speech or a heart-stirring sermon, but rather to a small book (fewer than seventy pages) entitled *Pia Desideria*, written by Philip Jacob Spener. This book was a call to church reformation and renewal, pointing people toward a return to a biblical and holy church. Its message spread quickly to Christians all over Europe, and its impact is almost inestimable.

John Wesley, the founder of Methodism, knew the power and influence of books. He was himself a prolific writer, the author of numerous books. Besides his own influential writings, he gathered together excerpts from the great Christian classics for use in training Methodist preachers. The early Methodist preachers were circuit riders who covered much territory on horseback, bringing the gospel to far-separated congregations. It is said that these preachers carried two saddlebags with them: one for clothes and one for the books that they distributed to their fellow believers. Wesley himself was a voracious reader. He covered untold miles on horseback, often riding without the reins so that he might read while he rode. Concerned that he might fall off his horse and hurt himself, some friends eventually provided him with a carriage. His first step was to have a bookcase built into it. This carriage not only provided more solitude for reading but was also much safer!

John Newton was the captain of a slave ship that transported human cargo across the seas. The experience of reading *The Imitation of Christ* by Thomas à Kempis changed his life and caused him to disown his inhuman occupation. Newton became a minister and is best known to us today as the author of the hymn "Amazing Grace." Similarly, it was a book by Philip Doddridge that awakened the soul and the conscience of Englishman William Wilberforce, who led the fight against the slave trade in England.

More recently, C. S. Lewis counted the reading of G. K. Chesterton's *Everlasting Man* and George MacDonald's *Phantastes* as key moments in his own pilgrimage toward faith. Lewis's own book *Mere Christianity* has played a major role in the lives of many searchers after the truth, including former presidential counsel Charles Colson.

For centuries books have always been powerful tools in awakening hearts, minds and consciences. Many of the people God has used most powerfully have been men and women who knew the value of good books.

It is the same for us today. Through the medium of great books we can not only be entertained but also expanded, transformed, informed and spiritually enlightened. Some of the most life-changing experiences in my own life came about through the reading of particular books, which seemed to bring just the message I needed to hear at key junctures in my life. I can promise you that time spent with some of the books introduced in this volume will not only bring you to a deeper awareness of the truth about God and faith but also deepen your perceptions about your own life. These books can serve as road maps on your own faith journey.

So enjoy!

TWO

WHY SHOULD I READ
THE CHRISTIAN CLASSICS?

With so many books to choose from in your local library or bookstore, why would anyone want to pass over the latest best-sellers or books on the hottest current topics to read one of the classics? Why spend time with books that are older than you are? Is it worth the effort it takes to read books that were written in distant times and cultures? How could they possibly be relevant to my life today? Basically, why should I read the Christian classics?

The simplest answer is this: the classic Christian books are worth reading because they are great books. They are books that have had a profound influence (sometimes consciously, sometimes not) on countless men and women down through the ages. What makes a book a classic is that it has proven itself by its impact, by the fact that, generation after generation, it continues to be relevant and rewarding to those who take the time to read and absorb it.

The classics are great because they change us intellectually and spiritually, affecting the way we think, feel and behave. They are a treasure bequeathed to us by some of our brothers and sisters in Christ who have gone before us.

In the church today there is an abysmal lack of awareness of the historical roots and the creative richness of our faith. Our cultural memory seems quite short. Many act, for all practical purposes, as if Christianity were invented by Billy Graham in the 1940s. And the only Calvin many Christians know is Calvin Klein or the mischievous young boy in the comic strip "Calvin and Hobbes." I heard about a Lutheran Sunday school teacher who, on Reformation Sunday, asked her students if they knew who Martin Luther was. Without hesitation, one young man raised his hand and said, "He's the black man who started our church." We are mostly ignorant of the men and women who had an important place in our history and who wrote books that have affected lives down through the centuries. But now, not only are the classic Christian books widely ignored, many are not even available in most Christian bookstores.

We have lost the sense of our heritage, of the glorious tradition we have as Christian believers. We tend to be too focused on today, ignoring the reality that the past has a continuing impact on the present. We need to learn to value the wisdom of Christians through the ages. (See appendix A for a discussion of the importance of tradition.)

Reading the Christian classics is one of the surest ways to broaden and deepen our faith and our commitment. I have found my own life to be immeasurably impacted by the great writers of the Christian tradition. Time spent with these classic books will help us to appreciate our diversity as believers as well as the creative and intellectual depth of our tradition; it will put us in touch with the perennial questions of humanity, the questions all human beings ask in their heart of hearts; it will introduce us to great minds, to the most profound and spiritually rich individuals who ever lived; it will give us a vantage point from which to critique the failings of our own time; and it will help us develop a more rounded and balanced Christian worldview.

Appreciating Our Diversity

There are a variety of expressions of the Christian faith—high-powered theologians and those who preach a simple gospel; pragmatists and mystics; solitaries and those who stress the social implications of the gospel; Arminians and Calvinists; Baptists and Catholics and Pentecostals. None of us has a corner on the truth. We can all learn something from each other. Reading the great Christian books helps us to appreciate this diversity within the body of Christ, both in our own time and in the past. Our differences may be real, but as we grow in an awareness of the variety of ideas and possible expressions of them within the Christian tradition, it may help us to see how few people there are in history with whom we can agree on every point. This helps to relativize our own sense of always being right about everything and causes us to focus instead on what C. S. Lewis called "mere Christianity"—the handful of essential ideas that distinguish Christianity from other faiths and ideologies.

As we read, we will discover several common themes that run throughout the great Christian writings and realize how much we can learn even from those with whom we have violent disagreements. For example, while Calvinists and Arminians may never fully agree about providence, free will and human freedom, Calvinists can learn to appreciate the penetrating insights of John Wesley, and Arminians, the rich thinking of John Calvin. In so doing, we might also find ourselves striking new positions of balance and tolerance. We can also much more clearly understand our own positions when we see them set up against the positions of others as articulated by our "adversaries" themselves.

As members of the body of Christ, we are not solo pianists or even a brass band playing in harmony. We are an orchestra. All our varying traditions and emphases work together to make the symphony that is the message of the Christian tradition.

Appreciating the Depth of Our Heritage

A wide reading in the Christian classics will demonstrate the depth and profundity of our tradition. Some critics accuse orthodox Christianity of being anticultural. But a tradition that can boast of the likes of Bach, Dostoyevsky, Rembrandt, Kierkegaard, Rouault, Pascal, Donne, Handel, Dante and Flannery O'Connor cannot fairly be dismissed as narrow, sterile or lacking in creative thrust.

We have a heritage in which we can take a proper sense of pride. Some of the finest artistic and creative achievements of all time have come from Christians.

Musicians such as Bach, Handel, Mozart, Stravinsky, Gorecki, Duke Ellington, Mark Heard and Bruce Cockburn.

Philosophers such as Aquinas, Pascal, Kierkegaard, Jacques Maritain, Gabriel Marcel and Alasdair MacIntyre.

Artists such as Giotto, Dürer, Michelangelo, Rembrandt, Caspar David Friedrich, Frederick Church, Van Gogh and Rouault.

Poets such as John Donne, George Herbert, Gerard Manley Hopkins, T. S. Eliot and Czeslaw Milosz.

And writers such as Dante, Shakespeare, Milton, Jane Austen, Dostoyevsky, Tolstoy, Tolkien, C. S. Lewis, Graham Greene, Walker Percy, Solzhenitsyn, Flannery O'Connor and Frederick Buechner.

Ours is a tradition of which we can be proud. We would do well to become better acquainted with it. The classic books are a great place to start.

Asking the Perennial Questions

Reading the great books can help us to understand how perennial the great questions of our faith are. Who is God? What is his role in human existence? What is humankind? What is our essential nature? What does the future hold? These books provide ever-new insights into these great questions. We can read them again and again, as they always seem to have something new to say to us, providing resources for the continued discussion of these issues. And because these works often disagree with one another, we will learn to read dialectically, with an open and questioning mind.

Our lives are so busy that we find ourselves focused only on what must be done this moment. We are consumed with the immediate, with our urgent needs, distracted from the solitude in which the questions of life can be contemplated. Unfortunately, the most important questions of life (purpose and meaning) are often the first thing to be ignored when life becomes harried. At the time we most need the truths found in the great questions, we tell ourselves that we don't have time to think on such things. If we do not ask these questions, we do not grow and learn. The great books confront us with important issues that demand a response.

Exposure to Great Minds

There used to be a program on public television called *Meeting of the Minds.*

The host, Steve Allen, would introduce guests from throughout history (of course they were really actors in costume) who would discuss great ideas and pressing concerns. A typical panel might consist of Martin Luther, Galileo, Albert Einstein and Socrates. Viewers enjoyed the program because they felt as if they had made a connection with some truly great thinkers.

In reading the classics we can have a similar experience—that of being ushered into the presence of some of the greatest thinkers and spiritually deepest women and men who ever lived. Reading these books allows us to carry on a conversation with them across time, to sit at the feet of people who loved God with passion and served him with abandon. We may not agree with everything they say. In fact, they often contradict one another. But we can learn more by arguing with them, thereby clarifying what we believe and why.

Of the hundred wisest people who ever lived, how many do you think are presently alive? One or two? Maybe as many as five? To learn from the wisest men and women we must make the effort to read their books. We can find mentors for ourselves among the saints who left their thoughts behind in their writings. How many truly deep people are in your circle of friends? You can expand that number by befriending the great books of our Christian heritage!

Seeing Beyond Today

Reading in the classics will also give us a perspective that is broader than the merely contemporary. In modern Christendom we are often prone to faddishness, placing our concerns in the ephemeral and transient rather than the weighty and eternal. We get caught up in debating issues like the interpretation of biblical prophecy, attempting to discern the signs of the last days and to "pin the tail on the antichrist." Working for many years in the Christian publishing business has given me some perspective on the way that theological fads come and go with alarming rapidity. Yesterday's burning issue becomes forgotten tomorrow as we dizzily chase the latest trends. A proper grounding in the great traditions of the church would help keep us on an even keel, making us properly skeptical of the "latest thinking" and keeping us focused on the critical essentials of the Christian faith.

Building a Christian Vision

These works are also valuable in that they can help us to understand that

Christianity is not just an abstract set of beliefs, but instead, a vision of reality. Sometimes we can get so wrapped up in defending the doctrinal assertions of our faith that we lose touch with the fact that the Christian faith is a comprehensive way of viewing the world, what Edith Schaeffer called "a way of seeing."

It is particularly in the works of fine art, poetry and fiction that are such a rich part of our heritage that we are provided with a creative vision for the world and our place within it. They demonstrate that the Christian will see his or her world in a different light from the nonbeliever. And this vision, as a sampling of these fine classic works will demonstrate, is marked by a realistic perspective about human limitations, a profound hope for change and betterment, and glorious promise that our lives make the most sense when they are seen in the light of eternity. Learning to communicate this aesthetic vision will make us more effective in our presentation of the gospel, as people are usually more deeply moved by a compelling vision of reality than they are by abstract intellectual argument.

Learning from the Past

Finally, the classics teach us about the mistakes and triumphs of those who have gone before us. These great books are not to be thought of as infallible sources of wisdom. They are, indeed, a record of much wisdom and insight. But they are also a record of false starts, wrong conclusions, human frailty and stubbornness. Just like us, these writers were fallen individuals whose own preconceptions and self-deceptions creep in. But even their mistakes can help us to see more clearly. Sometimes we can only fully discern the truth when we see it in juxtaposition with error. It is so easy to catch ourselves buying into ideas that represent what we *want* to believe to be true, rather than accepting the sometimes rather uncomfortable truth.

C. S. Lewis offered sage advice when he wrote, "It is a good rule, after reading a new book, never to allow yourself another new one till you have read an old one in between." His point was this: we need to connect with the wisdom of the past.

Don't be afraid to begin to explore. You'll soon come to realize that these books are not nearly as difficult as you may have come to believe. A few of them *are* difficult, and many will require a bit more concentration than modern books usually require. But these are books that have survived the test of time because of how well they communicate and how eternally relevant they are. And some are rich in humor, many are very entertaining, and all are worth the effort they may require.

I hope that the list of "The Great Books of the Christian Tradition" will help you begin or continue your own exploration of the valuable resources of our Christian heritage.

THREE

THE GREAT BOOKS
OF THE CHRISTIAN TRADITION

I n this chapter I've tried to isolate those books that have had the greatest continuing impact on the Christian faith. These are the books that have shaped the way we think and believe, or that have most artfully expressed the Christian vision of reality. Taken together, they represent the "communion of the saints" by way of ink and paper.

The Ancient World
In the first centuries after Christ, the church faced the challenge of developing a systematic presentation of the Christian gospel in a culture filled with competing religious systems. They left us a heritage of courageous proclamation and the wisdom that comes from close study of Scripture and prayerful surrender to God. We owe a great debt to these early believers.

THE BIBLE
In earlier times, it might have gone without saying that the Bible is the key book for understanding the mysteries of human nature and the reality of a sphere of existence beyond the purely material realm. Today some people see the Bible as merely a historical oddity; however, almost everyone would agree that it has had a profound influence on the way that people in the West view themselves and their world. The great literature of our culture is littered with references and allusions to the Bible. As one great critic put it, you cannot understand most of

the great literature of our civilization if you are not familiar with the Bible and with Shakespeare. The Bible's thoughts, ideas, personalities and phrases are the coin in which much of our cultural conversation is transacted.

To the eyes of faith, however, the Bible is much more: an inexhaustible source of wisdom and insight into the very mind of God. It is the Word of God. As St. Jerome wrote, "Ignorance of the Scriptures is ignorance of Christ." The Bible is the foundation for theology, a guide for the spiritual life, a foundation for ethics and a testimony to the power and grace of God in human history. The Bible should be read devotionally and studied intensely, and its teachings practiced faithfully.

There are many good modern translations. For accuracy I recommend the New International Version, the New American Standard Version or the New Revised Standard Version. For beauty there is no comparison to the rich poetic cadences of the King James Version.

THE APOSTOLIC FATHERS
Various collections of writings

The writings of the apostolic fathers give us a look at the church in its infancy. Many readers will be surprised to find how institutionalized the church was even in these early days, and how similar some of the issues they dealt with are to those issues still with us. Following are some of the writings of this group of early church leaders.

The Didache (author unknown; probably written in the middle of the second century) is a manual of church order and Christian ethics. It gives a fascinating look at the practice and the liturgy of the early church.

Both Clement (*Letter to the Corinthians,* ca. 96) and Ignatius (various letters, ca. 107) dwelt primarily on two issues: the necessity for loyalty to the bishops as God-ordained authority and the importance of avoiding doctrinal entrapment by the heretics who were abundant in those times.

Justin Martyr (100-165) was the first Christian apologist, one who argued the truth of Christianity against its pagan opponents. Unashamed, he made the case—opposing the intellectual elite of his day—that Christianity was the most rational of faiths. His fearless defense of the gospel eventually brought him the crown of a martyr when he refused to worship the state gods of Rome.

The Shepherd of Hermas (ca. 130) is a sort of extended parable, an account of the revelations made to Hermas by the church, which appears in the form of a woman; by a shepherd who represents repentance; and by a great angel. This book, very popular in the early church, is an allegory of sin, repentance and baptism.

Irenaeus (d. 202) also died a martyr. He is credited with being the first real theologian of the early church. In his works his powerful, logical mind is exercised in spelling out the key doctrines of the faith.

Tertullian (ca. 160-220) was one of the greatest of the Christian apologists. Though best known for his statement "I believe because it is absurd," he worked hard to show that Christianity should be accepted by the Roman Empire because the ethics and lifestyle of believers make them among the best of citizens.

The classic English translation of *The Apostolic Fathers* is that of J. B. Lightfoot. If you can locate a copy of the lively modern translation (with introductions and notes) by Jack Sparks, it will help to make the reading much easier.

ATHANASIUS (CA. 296-373)
On the Incarnation
Life of St. Antony

Athanasius has been long regarded as one of the most important and saintly theological thinkers of the early church. His contemporaries said of him that "he is a sincere, virtuous man, a good Christian, an ascetic, a true bishop." His key role in the Council of Nicea helped guard the church against the heresies that were so powerful in his time.

On the Incarnation is one of the keys works of the early church. In it, Athanasius attempts to give a rational explanation for the key Christian doctrine (the incarnation of God in Jesus Christ) and to elaborate on its meaning for the lives of believers. I especially recommend the edition published by SVS Press, which includes a marvelous preface by C. S. Lewis and a brief commentary on the Psalms by Athanasius, containing powerful spiritual insights on this important biblical book.

While *On the Incarnation* shows the theological acumen of Athanasius, the *Life of St. Antony* gives a glimpse of his spiritual insight as he writes one of the earliest spiritual biographies of the founder of the monastic way. This book teaches that the central occupation of the Christian life is the struggle to bring the flesh under control. Athanasius knew Antony personally and embraced the ascetic form of spirituality that Antony practiced, believing that only a life lived in holiness would open one's heart to God.

> You know how it is when some great king enters a large city and dwells in one of its houses; because of his dwelling in that single house, the whole city is honoured, and enemies and robbers cease to molest it. Even so is it with the King of all; He has come into our country and dwelt in one body amidst the many, and in consequence the designs of the enemy against mankind have been foiled, and the corruption of death, which formerly held them in its power, has simply ceased to be. For the human race would have perished utterly had not the Lord and Saviour of all, the Son of God, come among us to put an end to death.
>
> ST. ATHANASIUS, *On the Incarnation*

THE DESERT FATHERS
Various collections of writings

The desert fathers were forerunners of monasticism who left their lives in the cities and countryside to live as hermits or in small communities in the desert. The writings of the desert fathers consist of miracle stories, feats of incredible asceticism and, most important, penetrating insight into human nature. By leaving "the world" and looking inside themselves, they made many powerful discoveries.

The intriguing and often eccentric writings of these forerunners of the monastic tradition are filled with numerous examples of sly wisdom, an emphasis on negation of the self and a call to absolute surrender to God. At times these writings can seem strange and even a bit off-putting, but more often they burn white-hot with revelation about human limitations and the necessity of complete dedication to God. Thomas Merton has edited a lively collection of their writings under the title *The Wisdom of the Desert.* You may also find a helpful introduction to the spiritual riches of the desert fathers in Henri Nouwen's superb little book *The Way of the Heart.*

EUSEBIUS (CA. 260-339)
Ecclesiastical History

Eusebius is often called the father of church history—a title he earned by his extensive history of the Christian church during its first three centuries. Written in ten books over a period of fifteen years, it has stood the test of time. Most church historians agree that it is substantially accurate. Were it not for Eusebius, much of the history of the early church might remain largely unknown to us.

AUGUSTINE (345-430)
Confessions
The City of God

Augustine's *Confessions* is quite simply one of the greatest books ever written. It repays frequent rereading. Each time I read this book, it impresses me with new insights that I am surprised I did not discover on earlier readings. This searchingly honest autobiographical account of a soul in search of God will undoubtedly provoke soul searching on the part of any reader. It tells the story of Augustine's intellectual and spiritual journey through several major philosophies of his day, and of his awakening to the fact that only God could bring him freedom from the struggle with his flesh. Arguably the first real autobiography in Western culture, *Confessions* is written in the form of prayers of thanksgiving and praise to God. The exquisite beauty of Augustine's prose is well captured in the translations by R. S. Pine-Coffin and by Fulton Sheen.

The City of God is a much longer, more philosophical and historical book, and of much less interest to the casual reader, but it is an unquestionably important document in the development of a Christian view of history and culture. For those not prepared to tackle this very long book, it is still worth skimming. Augustine's doctrinal study, *On the Trinity*, is also recommended.

Peter Brown's *Augustine of Hippo* is an outstanding biography of Augustine that illuminates his many contributions to the Western intellectual and spiritual tradition.

I have learned to love you late, Beauty at once so ancient and so new! I have learned to love you late! You were within me, and I was in the world outside myself. I searched for you outside myself and, disfigured as I was, I fell upon the lovely things of your creation. You were with me, but I was not with you. The beautiful things of this world kept me far from you and yet, if they had not been in you, they would have had no being at all. You called me; you cried aloud to me; you broke my barrier of deafness. You shone upon me; your radiance enveloped me; you put my blindness to flight. You shed your fragrance about me; I drew breath and now I gasp for your sweet odor. I tasted you, and now I hunger and thirst for you. You touched me, and I am inflamed with love of your peace.
AUGUSTINE, *Confessions*

JOHN CHRYSOSTOM (CA. 347-407)
Sermons

Chrysostom, whose name means "golden mouth," was certainly that. In his day, he was known for his skill in preaching from the Scriptures in a way that was practical, beautiful, imaginative and intellectually compelling. In a time when the allegorical method was the most common way of approaching the Bible, Chrysostom urged a literal interpretation whenever possible. Because of this approach, his expository sermons on Genesis, Matthew, John and the Pauline epistles are still valuable and insightful today.

BENEDICT (CA. 480-543)
The Rule of St. Benedict

Benedict's rule can be credited with bringing a stabilizing influence to the monastic life. His rule is a short and insightful guide to the monastic life by the man who turned it into an organized system. Benedict built his view of the monastic life (a view that still prevails today) around three emphases: obedience to the hierarchy within the monastery, regular prayer and manual labor. What is still so striking about this rule is its sense of balance. While it contains enough strictness to help restrain the excesses of the flesh, it is also realistic enough about human nature not to be discouraging or overwhelmingly impossible to live by.

The Middle Ages

The very term "Middle Ages" is an indication of the way many people view this time period. For some, this period was simply the gap between the ancient and modern periods, a time of intellectual stagnation and mindless following of tradition. But such a characterization is not entirely fair, for while this may not have been a time of striking scientific innovation, it was certainly a time of great fertility in the Christian tradition. Though authority played its role as a steadying influence, much original and creative thinking and writing was taking place.

ANSELM OF CANTERBURY (CA. 1033-1109)
Monologium
Proslogium

These two important works of theology are concerned with building a logical case for the existence of God. Anselm's most notable achievement is the ontological proof for the existence of God. In brief, the ontological argument states that the fact that we are able to entertain the idea of God ("that than which nothing greater can be conceived") requires that God actually exist. In other words, if God did not objectively exist, we wouldn't even be able to imagine such a being. Whether or not you find this argument persuasive, especially in the oversimplified form I have just expressed it, it has been much debated and defended by theologians down through the years. One of the interesting characteristics of these two works is that they are written in the form of a series of prayers. The idea that theology can and should be done in the midst of prayer is certainly an appealing one.

BERNARD OF CLAIRVAUX (1090-1153)
On the Love of God
Sermons on the Song of Songs

Though Bernard was a very important man of his time, heavily involved in the religious and political struggles of his day, his writings reveal that he was also a man deeply in love with God. *On the Love of God* emphasizes God as the very basis and ground of love in all its forms. Bernard's sermons on the Song of Songs (better known today as the Song of Solomon) are an allegorical and mystical interpretation of this passionate biblical book. Jesus himself is the bridegroom, and we are the bride and the recipients of his overwhelming love. This is beautiful writing on God's passionate love for us, and an expression of deep personal devotion to the Savior.

Though written in a time often characterized by dry scholasticism, Bernard's books reveal a refreshingly sensual experience of God.

PETER ABELARD (1079-1142)
Letters of Abelard and Heloise

Abelard was one of the most famous and respected theological teachers of the Middle Ages. This collection of letters recounts his illicit romance with a young girl he was tutoring, which resulted in his castration (by order of the girl's angry father) and her forced exile to a convent.

Their tragic tale of temptation and guilt is honest and self-searching. While it reads with all the excitement of a modern novel, there is much profound reflection in these pages on human sin, the lure of illicit sexuality and a demonstration of forgiveness and the need for change.

FRANCIS OF ASSISI (1181-1226)
Little Flowers of St. Francis

The joyful tales about Francis and his followers are filled with wonder, sacrifice and devotion. These delightful and miraculous stories expound the exploits of Francis and his band of followers. Readers will likely find themselves overwhelmed by Francis's childlike trust and simplicity of heart, and by his resulting spiritual power. One quickly senses why he was one of the great spiritual leaders of all time and why the devotion to his simple message still lives on. Francis was perhaps one of the most Christlike men who ever lived. Read G. K. Chesterton's *St. Francis* for a loving but unsentimental retelling of his life.

> Lord, make me an instrument of Thy peace;
>> where there is hatred, let me sow love;
>> where there is injury, pardon;
>> where there is doubt, faith;
>> where there is despair, hope;
>> where there is darkness, light;
>> and where there is sadness, joy.
> O Divine Master,
>> grant that I may not so much seek

to be consoled as to console;
to be understood as to understand;
to be loved as to love;
for it is in giving that we receive,
it is in pardoning that we are pardoned,
and it is in dying that we are born to eternal life. FRANCIS OF ASSISI

THOMAS AQUINAS (CA. 1225-1274)
Summa Theologica

Aquinas was one of the most profound and prolific thinkers of all time. During his life he covered enough pages with his carefully considered words to fill over one hundred volumes. His masterwork was the *Summa Theologica*, a massive work of theology that itself fills a number of volumes. Aquinas's lifelong goal was to bring faith and reason together. He taught that the Christian faith is not inherently opposed to the life of the mind, and he worked hard to show that faith can be defended, and its opponents rebutted, by reason. In reading his work, one is struck by its careful logic, its fairness to those he disagrees with and its deep loyalty to Scripture and church tradition. This book is the benchmark of Catholic theology.

If you don't want to try to tackle the whole thing (its length is certainly intimidating!), an excellent place to begin is the condensation with notes by Peter Kreeft, entitled *Summa of the Summa*.

DANTE ALIGHERI (1265-1321)
La Vita Nuova
The Divine Comedy

Dante's masterpiece, *The Divine Comedy*, is the story of a mythical journey through hell, purgatory and paradise. The attentive reader absorbs theological learning, political satire and engaging drama in one of the greatest books of all time. The writing is beautiful, and Dante is passionate about what he believes. While a book for the ages, it is also a book rooted in its time. Dante is unsparing in his criticism of corruption and unrighteousness, especially as seen in the church hierarchy. In fact, he denounced many contemporary church leaders, placing them in his fictionalized hell.

I highly recommend the very fine annotated translation by John Ciardi.

Also worth noting is the vivid translation by Dorothy L. Sayers.

Dante's earlier work, *La Vita Nuova (The New Life)*, is a poetic meditation on the nature of romantic love and its relationship to divine love. It introduces us to the beautiful Beatrice, who plays the role of his guide through heaven in *The Divine Comedy*. In *La Vita Nuova* his love for her awakens within him a love for God.

> Midway in our life's journey, I went astray
> > from the straight road and woke to find myself
> > alone in a dark wood. How shall I say
> what wood that was! I never saw so drear,
> > so rank, so arduous a wilderness!
> > Its very memory gives a shape to fear.
> Death could scarce be more bitter than that place!
> > But since it came to good I will recount
> > all that I found revealed there by God's grace. DANTE ALIGHERI, *Inferno*

AUTHOR UNKNOWN
The Cloud of Unknowing

This important mystical treatise centers on the incomprehensibility of God and our inability to capture an understanding of him through the limited resources of our human conceptions. God, says the anonymous author, dwells beyond all our concepts in a divine "dazzling darkness." Many will feel the author goes too far at points, but this is a healthy corrective to the cocksure theology that claims to fully comprehend the person and plan of God. A little mystery can be a very healthy thing.

RICHARD ROLLE (CA. 1300-1349)
The Fire of Love

Rolle left Oxford University at age nineteen to become a hermit. His experience of God's presence as a rapturous and life-transforming warmth in his heart changed his life forever. In lyrical and often alliterative prose Rolle celebrates the intoxicating love of God. He emphasizes that God can best be known not through the efforts of the human mind, but through a heart that is touched by the Savior. The translation by M. L. del Mastro preserves the beauty of Rolle's prose style.

JULIANA OF NORWICH (1343-1413)
Revelations of Divine Love

Through the revelations that Juliana was given by God, she reflects meditatively on the nurturing, "feminine" side of God and upon God's all-encompassing love and mercy. One should not, however, confuse her meditations on God's mothering actions in our lives with the feminist or goddess theology that has become so prevalent in recent years. What Juliana is pointing to is God's role as both mother and father in the lives of believers. Writing at a time when the sternness and unapproachability of God were emphasized, Juliana brings balance with this vision of God's incomprehensible love, grace and mercy. When we know him in whom we place our trust, as Juliana writes, "All shall be well and all shall be well and all manner of things shall be well."

> And in this God showed me something small, not bigger than a hazelnut, lying in the palm of my hand, as it seemed to me, and it was round as a ball. I looked at it with the eye of my understanding and thought: What can this be? I was amazed that it could last for I thought that because of its littleness, it would surely have fallen into nothing. And I was answered in my understanding: It lasts, and always will, because God loves it; and thus everything has being through the love of God. JULIANA OF NORWICH, *Revelations of Divine Love*

GEOFFREY CHAUCER (CA. 1343-1400)
The Canterbury Tales

This collection of tales, sometimes profound, sometimes bawdy, ranges over many aspects of human existence. Chaucer gives us a collection of stories told by a group of pilgrims to while away the passing miles on their way to the church at Canterbury. The stories are by turns amusing, moving, heroic, tragic, sensual and inspirational. Here is truly "all God's plenty" in his human creation: the good, the bad, the honest, the despicable and the holy. It is a marvelous cornucopia of stories.

Those who question the faith of Chaucer (whom some modern critics have suggested was an agnostic) should look again at his epilogue, where he dedicates both the work and his life to God. The original Old English text is recommended only for the diligent and adventurous. For most people a modern translation will make the book more enjoyable.

CATHERINE OF SIENNA (1347-1380)
The Spiritual Dialogue

One of the most striking things about Catherine of Sienna was her balance of the active and the contemplative life. From her youngest days she had a deeply experiential relationship with God and sometimes found herself lost in mystical rapture. By the age of twenty, however, she had dedicated her life to caring for the sick, especially those suffering from diseases that most people found repugnant. Although a mystic, her life of contemplation was balanced by a life of sacrificial service. Her holiness was so obvious that rulers of both church and state came to her for advice and spiritual guidance.

In *The Spiritual Dialogue* she describes the pathway to holiness for the believer, emphasizing the "Precious Blood of Christ" as the surest evidence of God's love for us. The balance of her life is evident in her writings as she emphasizes that God primarily uses normal, ordinary people as the channels of his love and grace.

THOMAS À KEMPIS (CA. 1380-1471)
The Imitation of Christ

One of the bestselling books of all time, this devotional classic is marked by its call for single-minded devotion to Jesus Christ and a simple, uncluttered life of adoration. Thomas à Kempis calls us to imitate Christ's life and to practice his teachings with humility and trust in the grace of God. Within these pages are some of the most heart-stirring and convicting passages in all of devotional literature. One of the most sane and balanced of all the mystics, à Kempis has, through this book, deeply influenced the lives of countless believers.

Do not try to read the book too quickly or digest too much of it at one time. Some people have found it repetitive, but that is part of its art. If you read in small doses, you will find à Kempis returning again and again to his main themes. The cumulative force is challenging and transforming. It is a book to be savored, prayed over and meditated upon.

> What good can it do you to discuss the mystery of God in the Trinity in learned terms if you lack humility and so displease that God? Learned arguments do not make a man holy and righteous, whereas a good life makes him dear to God. I would rather feel compunction in my heart than be able to define it. If you knew the whole Bible by heart and all the expositions of scholars, what good would it

do you without the love and grace of God?

THOMAS À KEMPIS, *The Imitation of Christ*

The Early Modern World

In the Christian tradition the Reformation was the key event of this period. The era we know as the Renaissance was characterized by a freedom of intellectual inquiry and a growing sense of individualism, the belief that each person is unique and important. In the area of religious faith this produced a willingness to question the traditional church authority, a renewed search for the individual experience of God's grace and a desire to probe deeply into the hard realities of the human condition. Out of this period came some of the most profound works of Western history in theology, philosophy and literature.

MARTIN LUTHER (1483-1546)
The Freedom of the Christian
The Bondage of the Will
Table Talk

The great Reformer writes powerfully of salvation by faith alone and the power of grace. His theological works are seminal for understanding the history of theology, and his *Table Talk* reveals something of Luther the man: his brilliance, devotion and sense of humor. Two of the better recent biographies are those of Roland Bainton *(Here I Stand)* and Heiko Oberman *(Luther: Man Between God and the Devil).*

Nothing makes a man good except faith, nor evil except unbelief.

It is indeed true that in the sight of men a man is made good or evil by his works, but this being made good or evil is no more than that he who is good or evil is pointed out and known as such.

He, therefore, who does not wish to go astray with those blind men, must look beyond works, and laws and doctrines about works; nay, turning his eyes from works, he must look upon the person, and ask how that is justified. For the person is justified and saved not by works nor by laws, but by the Word of God, that is, by the promise of His grace, and by faith, that the glory may remain God's, Who saved us not by works of righteousness which we have done, but according to His mercy by the word of His grace, when we believed.

MARTIN LUTHER, *A Treatise on Christian Liberty*

IGNATIUS OF LOYOLA (1491-1556)
Spiritual Exercises

A book of devotions and guided meditations for the development of the spiritual life. One of the methods that Ignatius suggests is the exercise of imagining yourself present at the events recorded in the Gospels. Many moderns have found this guide still useful in the twentieth century.

JOHN CALVIN (1509-1564)
Institutes of the Christian Religion

Calvin is the other great Reformer and a man of penetrating intelligence. His *Institutes* are indisputably one of the most important of all works of theology. They evidence his attempt to formulate a logical and systematic presentation of all the areas of theology. Comparing Calvin's writings with the popular conception of Calvinism might prove an eye-opening experience for many readers.

> Our wisdom, in so far as it ought to be deemed true and solid wisdom, consists almost entirely of two parts—the knowledge of God and of ourselves. But as these are connected together by many ties, it is not easy to determine which of the two precedes and gives birth to the other. For, in the first place, no man can survey himself without forthwith turning his thought toward the God in whom he lives and moves.
>
> The miserable ruin into which the revolt of the first man has plunged us compels us to turn our eyes upwards.
>
> Since nothing appears within us or around us which is not tainted with very great impurity, so long as we keep our mind within the confines of human pollution, anything which is in some small degree less defiled delights us as if it were most pure. JOHN CALVIN, *Institutes of the Christian Religion*

TERESA OF ÁVILA (1515-1582)
Interior Castle
The Life of St. Teresa

A Spanish nun and mystic, Teresa's work is characterized by a deep devotion and a strong streak of practicality. Hers is a mysticism that can be practiced by the common woman or man. Note especially her warnings against false forms of spiritual experience. *Interior Castle* is a wise book on the inner life by a wise woman. *The Life of St. Teresa* is her autobiography.

JOHN OF THE CROSS (1542-1591)

The Dark Night of the Soul
The Ascent of Mt. Carmel

John of the Cross was a Spanish mystic with a poetic soul and a deep insight into the realities of the Christian experience. He is searchingly honest about the difficulties and ambiguities of the walk of faith. Though his books are not easy to read, they are worth the effort it takes to read them slowly and with an open heart. They are essential reading for understanding the deeper forms of Christian mysticism.

WILLIAM SHAKESPEARE (1546-1616)

King Lear
The Merchant of Venice
Romeo and Juliet
Henry IV, Parts 1 and 2
Hamlet
Macbeth
Othello

Whatever the circumstances of his personal life (and these are hidden in the fogs of history), it is unquestionably true that Shakespeare wrote from a Christian worldview. His insights on human will, guilt, forgiveness, and the search for truth should be required reading for every believer. His grasp of the human condition is perhaps unmatched in literature. If read seriously, his work can be used as a mirror through which we can see ourselves. As the great critic Harold Bloom wrote, "He perceived more than any other writer, thought more profoundly and originally than any other, and had an almost effortless mastery of language, far surpassing everyone."

LANCELOT ANDREWES (1555-1626)

Private Devotions

These are the lovely poetic meditations of an Anglican cleric, whose beautiful style was instrumental in the creation of the *Book of Common Prayer*. A cadence at once both lofty and heartfelt is struck in this series of devotional prayers.

FRANCIS DE SALES (1567-1622)
Introduction to the Devout Life

This book offers advice on holy living that influenced generations of Protestants and Catholics alike. It was one of C. S. Lewis's favorite pieces of devotional writing. Within its pages you'll find a treasure trove of spiritual gems. His book does not emphasize some sort of otherworldly mysticism; instead, it offers a practical and challenging guide to spiritual growth.

JOHN DONNE (1575-1631)
Sermons
Poems

Don't miss the well-crafted work of this master of the English language. His poems manage to crystallize spiritual experiences and communicate the drama of an encounter with God in a way seldom captured in any religious poetry. The place to begin is with his *Holy Sonnets*. His sermons are also beautiful and insightful.

> Batter my heart, three-personed God; for You
> As yet but knock, breathe, shine, and seek to mend;
> That I may rise, and stand, overthrow me, and bend
> Your force, to break, blow, burn and make me new.
> I, like a usurped town, to another due,
> Labor to admit You but Oh, to no end!
> Reason, Your viceroy in me, should defend,
> But it is captive, and proves weak or untrue.
> Yet dearly I love You, and would be loved fain.
> But am betrothed unto Your enemy;
> Divorce me, untie, or break that knot again,
> Take me to You, imprison me, for I
> Except You enthrall me, never shall be free,
> Nor ever chaste, except You ravish me. JOHN DONNE, *Holy Sonnets*

GEORGE HERBERT (1593-1633)
Poems

Herbert wrote many deceptively simple, honest and beautiful poems, mostly about the spiritual life. One of the strengths of Herbert's poetry is that he does not, as many religious poets do, tell us how we *should* feel, but rather is honest about the struggles we all face. Throughout his writings, his love for the Savior is unmistakable.

> Love bade me welcome; yet my soul drew back,
>   Guilty of dust and sin.
> But quick-eyed love, observing me grow slack
>   From my first entrance in,
> Drew nearer to me, sweetly questioning,
>   If I lacked any thing.
> A guest, I answered, worthy to be here;
>   Love said, You shall be he.
> I the unkind, ungrateful? Ah my dear,
>   I cannot look on thee.
> Love took my hand, and smiling did reply,
>   Who made the eyes but I?
> Truth Lord, but I have marred them: let my shame
>   Go where it doth deserve.
> And know you not says Love, who bore the blame?
>   My dear then I will serve.
> You must sit down, says Love, and taste my meat;
>   So I did sit down and eat. GEORGE HERBERT, "Love"

JOHN MILTON (1608-1674)
Paradise Lost
Poems

The great epic poem *Paradise Lost* is a bold, dramatic re-creation of the fall of man. Certainly one of the most important poems of all time, it has been influential in creating some of our popular cultural conceptions of God and the devil. His insights into the psychology of evil are perhaps unmatched in all literature.

BROTHER LAWRENCE (1611-1691)
The Practice of the Presence of God

These are the writings of a simple monk who learned to live moment by moment in the presence of God despite the distractions of life. It is a life-transforming work that stresses the reality of relationship with the living

God. I have read this book many times and always found it a powerful spiritual tonic to the distractions of my life.

RICHARD BAXTER (1615-1691)
The Saints' Everlasting Rest

The great Puritan writer calls us to form our lives in recognition of the life hereafter, a life only available to those who trust completely in the grace of God. Baxter has written a work of concrete hope based on the promises and character of God.

BLAISE PASCAL (1623-1662)
Pensées

Pensées is the French word for "thoughts," and these are what comprise this collection of writings. Pascal spent years gathering thoughts in preparation for a book on the truth of the Christian faith. He died before the book could be published, but he left behind this compilation of jottings on the nature of man, the reality of God and the paradox of faith—issues so current that the book reads as though it could have been written yesterday. An intelligent book on the limits of reason and the necessity of faith, it is one of the truly indispensable works of the Christian tradition.

> Reason's last step is the recognition that there are an infinite number of things which are beyond it. It is merely feeble if it does not go as far as to realize that.
>
> The heart has reasons of which reason knows nothing.
>
> Knowing God without knowing our own wretchedness makes for pride. Knowing our wretchedness without knowing God makes for despair. Knowing Jesus Christ strikes the balance because he shows us both God and our own wretchedness. BLAISE PASCAL, *Pensées*

GEORGE FOX (1624-1691)
George Fox: An Autobiography

The journal of this great Quaker social activist and spiritual leader contains an important challenge to readers today. His life is an example of how powerful one man's life can be when he devotes himself to living by the principles of Jesus Christ, even when this goes against the flow of the prevailing religious establishment.

JOHN BUNYAN (1628-1688)
The Pilgrim's Progress

One of the most-loved books of all time, *The Pilgrim's Progress* is an allegorical story that parallels the journey of faith of the Christian. It is filled with argument and theology, but rewards even the casual reader because of its drama. Many of its images are unforgettable; its vision of the Christian life is realistic in its evocation of struggle but ultimately filled with great hope. Since it was written, it has been read and reread by Christians of all persuasions.

> Christian ran thus till he came to a place somewhat ascending; and upon that place stood a cross and a little below in the bottom, a sepulcher. So I saw in my dream, that just as Christian came up with the cross, his burden loosed from off his shoulders and fell from off his back, and began to tumble and so continued to do till it came to the mouth of the sepulcher, where it fell in and I saw it no more.
> JOHN BUNYAN, *The Pilgrim's Progress*

PHILIP JACOB SPENER (1635-1705)
Pia Desideria

These are Puritan reflections on the life of faith. Spener argues that the church needs reformation and that this will only come through a renewed emphasis on the Bible, the priesthood of all believers, true Christian lifestyle and holiness among the clergy. This sounds like a good prescription for today's church.

THOMAS TRAHERNE (1637-1674)
Centuries of Meditations

Prose poems that show evidence of deep faith and an appreciation for nature as the creation of God. Traherne sees the majesty of God filling and enriching all of creation. This book, largely forgotten, deserves to be better known. In my opinion it contains some of the most beautiful writing in the English language. It is also wonderfully inspiring.

> You never enjoy the world aright, till you see how a grain of sand exhibiteth the wisdom and power of God, and prize in every thing the service which they do to you in manifesting His glory and goodness to your soul far more than the visible beauty of their surface, or the material services they can do your body.
> Your enjoyment of the world is never right till every morning you awake in

your Father's palace and look upon the skies and the earth and the air as celestial
joys having such a reverend esteem of all, as if you were among the angels. The
bride of a monarch, in her husband's chamber, hath no such causes of delight as
you. THOMAS TRAHERNE, *Centuries of Meditations*

MADAME (JEANNE) GUYON (1648-1717)
Experiencing the Depths of Jesus Christ

Madame Guyon, a French aristocrat, penned this guide to prayer that
emphasizes the necessity of self-abnegation and radical abandonment to the
will of God. It is a key work of the Quietist school of spirituality and has
influenced many contemporary mystics.

FRANCIS FÉNELON (1651-1715)
Christian Perfection

Fénelon is a French spiritual writer who discusses all phases of the spiritual
life, with a focus on humility and trust in God to transform our lives. His
advice was much sought after and cherished in his own time, and his wise
words remain powerful today.

DANIEL DEFOE (1660-1731)
Robinson Crusoe

An engaging and exciting story, this is the famous novel of a shipwrecked
man who has to learn to cope with life outside civilization. In his struggle to
survive, Crusoe learns the necessity of trust in the providence of God to
care for him.

The Eighteenth Century

*These years brought about the first concentrated challenge to the earlier domi-
nance of Christianity in the intellectual sphere. Enlightenment thinkers did
not flinch from bringing the truths of the Scriptures into question. Christian
thinkers, meanwhile, tended to turn inward, focusing on the interior life. The
majority of the Christian works of this period emphasize the relationship of the
individual believer with Christ. Christians were experiencing a time of revival,
renewal and spiritual refreshment, even in the face of this intellectual struggle.
However, the failure to adequately address the objections raised during this time*

may be the reason for the gradual decline in the cultural impact of Christianity.

JONATHAN SWIFT (1667-1745)
Gulliver's Travels

Swift was a cleric with an acerbic wit. In *Gulliver's Travels* he demonstrates his skepticism about the perfectibility of human nature. Though one can read this book simply as an exciting adventure tale, it is much more than that. Swift can also be read as a critic of the new Enlightenment ideas that were sweeping Europe in his time. He lays bare the corrupt nature of humankind and its moral inadequacy for designing a society based on reason and order. Swift's other satiric tales, including *A Modest Proposal* and *Battle of the Books,* further demonstrate his great intelligence and caustic sense of humor.

JEAN PAUL DE CAUSSADE (CA. 1675-1751)
Abandonment to Divine Providence

A small gem of a book, expressing a deep trust of God's sovereign superintendence over our lives. Every moment, says Caussade, is a sacred opportunity to allow God to shape and change us by the experiences that come our way. The spirit of the book is captured well in Kitty Muggeridge's translation entitled *The Sacrament of the Present Moment.*

WILLIAM LAW (1686-1761)
A Serious Call to the Devout and Holy Life

A classic Anglican work of devotion, *A Serious Call* is characterized by its levelheadedness and practicality. C. S. Lewis is among those who saw this book as one of the handful of truly great books on spiritual living.

JONATHAN EDWARDS (1703-1758)
Treatise on Religious Affections

One of the most important theologians of the eighteenth century, Edwards writes memorably on the place of emotions in the spiritual life. As with his other works, this book is characterized by a deep reliance on Scripture and a systematic intelligence. Many have argued that Edwards was one of the most brilliant minds that the United States has ever produced. Along with his powerful sermons, Edwards also produced books on practical spirituality and on philosophy. There has been a resurgence of interest from the academic community in Edwards's careful philosophical writings. Edwards's heart, however, was always fired by a passion for the revival of vigorous faith in the heart of the believer. John Gerstner has produced a slim, readable volume outlining Edwards's theological system for those new to his thought.

> As in worldly things worldly affections are very much the spring of men's motions and action; so in religious matters the spring of their actions is very much religious affections. He that has doctrinal knowledge and speculation only, without affection, never is engaged in the business of religion. Nothing is more manifest, in fact, than that the things of religion take hold of men's souls no further than they affect them.
> JONATHAN EDWARDS, *Treatise on Religious Affections*

JOHN WESLEY (1703-1791)
The Journals of John Wesley

Probably the best source for understanding the thought and motivations of the founder of Methodism. Wesley broke through much of the dry scholasticism of his time and emerged with a faith based on a "heart strangely warmed." The impact of his thought on evangelical Christians has been profound, especially, of course, on those of the Wesleyan tradition.

> In the evening I went very unwillingly to a society in Aldersgate Street, where one was reading Luther's preface to the Epistle to the Romans. About a quarter before nine, while he was describing the change which God works in the heart through faith in Christ, I felt my heart strangely warmed. I felt I did trust Christ alone, for salvation. And an assurance was given me that he had taken away my sins, even mine, and saved me from the law of sin and death.
> JOHN WESLEY, *The Journals of John Wesley*

DAVID BRAINERD (1718-1747)
The Life and Diary of David Brainerd

This is the stirring diary of a true man of prayer. A missionary to Native Americans, Brainerd was effective in part due to the astonishing amount of time he spent on his knees. A book guaranteed to awaken an awareness of our own lack of prayer and to call us to spend more time communicating with God.

WILLIAM BLAKE (1757-1827)
Songs of Innocence and of Experience

Though his theological outlook was not always orthodox, Blake's poetry contains a vigorous evocation of the difference that having eyes of faith makes in viewing the world. His poetry is, at times, disarmingly simple on the surface but is constructed around a deeply held belief in an order beyond the world of things. Blake's poetry was truly original and has proven influential on succeeding generations.

The Nineteenth Century

This was a period of great challenges to the church. In response to attacks from prominent intellectuals (for example, Marx, Comte, Nietzsche) and the general feeling that Christianity was becoming irrelevant, Christian thinkers struggled to make their faith intelligible to the modern mind. Many reformulated the gospel to make it more acceptable to its despisers, thus giving birth to liberal theology. Others emphasized the emotional promise of the gospel or wedded it to political agendas. Still others met the challenge by engaging the modern mind in new and creative ways while remaining faithful to "the faith once delivered."

FRIEDRICH SCHLEIERMACHER (1768-1834)
On Religion: Speeches to Its Cultured Despisers

Schleiermacher attempted to communicate Christianity to his peers in the Romantic movement, and to describe the life of faith in a way that could be grasped without recourse to dogmatic theological statements. Both his conception of religion as "the feeling of absolute dependence" and his theological method have had a profound effect on liberal theology. His prose, however, is dense and difficult.

SAMUEL TAYLOR COLERIDGE (1772-1834)
Poems
Aids to Reflection

One of the leaders of the Romantic movement, a literary critic and amateur theologian as well as a poet, Coleridge is a figure to be reckoned with. He was a convert to Christianity, and his poems often demonstrate an interest in the things of the spirit. *Aids to Reflection* contains some of his most focused spiritual writing.

JANE AUSTEN (1775-1817)
Pride and Prejudice
Emma

Austen's novels of manners advance high moral ideals but without stooping to preachiness or sentimentalism. Austen was a keen observer of human relationships; her writing displays a deep distrust of the kind of romantic love celebrated in our modern films and books.

CHARLES FINNEY (1792-1875)
Lectures on Revivals of Religion

An important forerunner of the evangelical movement, Finney called for a commitment that was radical and wholehearted. He recognized the important place of emotions in the Christian life but was, most of all, utterly committed to the Bible and its message.

JOHN HENRY NEWMAN (1801-1890)
Apologia Pro Vita Sua

This is the beautifully written story of Newman's conversion from Anglicanism to Catholicism. Newman was an astute theologian and one of the most important Catholic thinkers of modern times. In addition to this book, you might explore his profound musings on education.

NIKOLAI GOGOL (1809-1852)
Short Stories
Dead Souls

Gogol wrote rather strange and nightmarish stories about the human inability to make sense of an absurd world. Himself a believer, he had tremendous insight into the hollowness of a society constructed without God.

ROBERT BROWNING (1812-1889)
Poems

The intensity of Browning's faith shows itself in many of his poems. He is the rare poet who can write of spiritual things in such a way that they communicate even to the unbeliever.

SØREN KIERKEGAARD (1813-1855)
Either/Or
Fear and Trembling
Sickness unto Death
Training in Christianity
The Attack upon Christendom

One of the most profound thinkers of modern times, Kierkegaard saw the human predicament clearly: that human beings could not find the meaning and depth of their existence by the use of reason alone. Rather, it is only the life of faith that allows us to reach our full personhood and to give our lives purpose. This faith must be one of absolute commitment, even when it appears irrational. One cannot overstate Kierkegaard's influence on thinkers of various stripes. A good introduction to his sometimes difficult thought is Robert Bretall's *A Kierkegaard Anthology,* which includes excellent notes. Kierkegaard's sermons are also worth exploring. To learn about the strange life and preoccupations of this thinker, consult Walter Lowrie's readable biography, *A Short Life of Kierkegaard.*

> The thing is to understand myself, to see what God really wishes me to do; the thing is to find a truth which is really true for me, and to find the idea for which I can live and die.
>
> What good would it do me to be able to explain the meaning of Christianity if it had no deeper significance for me and for my life;—what good would it do me if truth stood before me, cold and naked, not caring whether I recognized her or not, and producing in me a shudder of fear rather than a trusting devotion?
> SØREN KIERKEGAARD, *The Journals of Søren Kierkegaard*

ANTHONY TROLLOPE (1815-1882)
The Warden
Barchester Towers

These charming tales of rural clerical life show keen insight into human nature. Both touching and humorous, these books are only the first two in a series of novels about the politics of an English parish. Pastors and priests will recognize how little things have changed when it comes to the internal battles of church politics.

ANONYMOUS RUSSIAN MONK
The Way of a Pilgrim

A key work of the Russian spiritual tradition, this spiritual journal teaches the use of the Jesus Prayer, a way of "praying unceasingly." This spiritual discipline has influenced countless believers in the Orthodox tradition and elsewhere.

FYODOR DOSTOYEVSKY (1821-1881)
The Underground Man
Crime and Punishment
The Idiot
The Brothers Karamazov

Dostoyevsky is quite possibly the greatest novelist of all time. His novels, especially *The Brothers Karamazov,* deal with the full gamut of human emotions and religious experience. He struggles with an array of intellectual and spiritual issues, but never lets the story itself bog down. Dostoyevsky's writing demonstrates a haunting awareness of the depths to which human beings can sink and the heights of self-sacrifice of which we are capable. And he tells it all with a passion that puts most other novelists to shame. Here is the Christian worldview demonstrated at its most profound with passages of awe-inspiring tenderness and passion.

> The awful thing is that beauty is mysterious as well as terrible. God and the devil are fighting there, and the battlefield is the heart of man.
> FYODOR DOSTOYEVSKY, *The Brothers Karamazov*

GEORGE MACDONALD (1824-1903)

Fairy Tales

Lilith

At the Back of the North Wind

Thomas Wingfold, Curate

With a romantic's zest for life and appreciation of nature, and a childlike sense of the truly important, George MacDonald presents a view of human life that is perhaps most notable for its rich sense of holiness. All of his writings reveal a man in love with his present existence who, at the same time, longs for eternity. Despite their occasional literary imperfections, his fairy tales and novels contain many of the most powerful moments of spiritual insight in literature. MacDonald deeply influenced later writers such as C. S. Lewis. Both Michael Phillips and Roland Hein have written interesting biographical studies, and Hein's literary study, *The Harmony Within,* is indispensable. Most of MacDonald's charming novels have been edited for contemporary readers by Michael Phillips and assigned new titles.

LEO TOLSTOY (1828-1910)

War and Peace

Anna Karenina

The Death of Ivan Ilyich

My Confession

Short Stories

Tolstoy and Dostoyevsky are the two giants of Russian literature. Tolstoy's ability to create memorable characters and to graphically show how real change takes place within the hearts and souls of his characters are two of the many things that make his novels so great. Short-story parables such as "How Much Land Does a Man Need?" or "Master and Man" are a good place to begin exploring the world of Tolstoy. Although his personal theology was less than orthodox, he saw deeply into the failures of humankind, especially as compared with the model given by Jesus Christ. *My Confession* is a powerful book about his own spiritual journey and religious awakening.

CHARLES SPURGEON (1834-1892)
John Ploughman's Talks
Sermons

One of the greatest masters of the pulpit with a brilliant mind and dedication to the Scriptures, Spurgeon could hold audiences spellbound with his rhetoric, his metaphors and his intense passion for lost souls. All these can be seen and experienced in his sermons and writings.

GERARD MANLEY HOPKINS (1844-1889)
Poems

Hopkins had a keen eye for the beauties of nature and the ability to use his mastery of the English language to produce beautiful poetry. Characterized by his desire to glimpse into the very nature of things (which he called "inscape"), Hopkins's work employs a striking juxtaposition of words to produce a rhythm that gives the poems their originality. He is one of my favorite poets.

> The world is charged with the grandeur of God.
>   It will flame out, like shining from shook foil;
>   It gathers to a greatness, like the ooze of oil
> Crushed. Why do men then now not reck his rod?
> Generations have trod, have trod, have trod;
>   And all is seared with trade, bleared, smeared with toil;
>   And wears man's smudge and shares man's smell: the soil
> Is bare now, nor can foot feel, being shod.
> And for all this, nature is never spent;
>   There lives the dearest freshness deep down things;
> And though the last lights off the black west went
>   Oh morning, at the brown brink eastward, springs—
> Because the Holy Ghost over the bent
>   World broods with warm breast and with ah! bright wings.
> GERARD MANLEY HOPKINS, "God's Grandeur"

CHARLES SHELDON (1857-1946)
In His Steps

In this popular novel a church undertakes a life-changing experiment: making no choices in life without first asking, "What would Jesus do?" If you can overlook its tendency toward quaintness, you'll find the results of this experiment make for truly inspiring and challenging reading.

FRANCIS THOMPSON (1859-1907)
Poems

Thompson finds a place on this list largely on the strength of his remarkable poem "The Hound of Heaven," which provides an unforgettable picture of God's passionate pursuit of the human soul. God's love causes him never to despair of us or give up on us.

> I fled Him, down the nights and down the days;
> I fled Him, down the arches of the years;
> I fled Him, down the labyrinthine ways
>   Of my own mind; and in the mist of tears
> I hid from Him, and under running laughter.
>   Up vistaed hopes I sped;
>   And shot, precipitated,
> Adown Titanic glooms of chasmed fears,
> From those strong Feet that followed,
>   followed after.
> FRANCIS THOMPSON, "The Hound of Heaven"

AMY CARMICHAEL (1867-1951)
If

Carmichael dedicated her life to improving the lot and saving the souls of young girls forced into temple prostitution in India. Much of the simple love and trust that marked her life is also demonstrated in her writing, like this book of simple but profound meditations. Elisabeth Elliot's biography of her *(A Chance to Die)* is valuable for understanding her accomplishments.

THÉRÈSE OF LISIEUX (1873-1897)
The Story of a Soul

The simple and tender story of a very young French nun whose love for God knew no bounds. Although some may find elements of her story (her extreme asceticism, for example) off-putting, no one can help but be struck by her passion for and devotion to the Lord Jesus Christ. "The little flower," as she is commonly known, has become one of the most popular of modern saints.

OSWALD CHAMBERS (1874-1917)
My Utmost for His Highest

This book of daily devotional readings has continued to find new readers well into our own time. Chambers's powerful reflections are based on deep evangelical experience and a close study of the Scriptures. Jim Reiman has created a modernized version of this classic devotional.

The Twentieth Century and Beyond

As people in modern times have lost confidence in absolute truth, Christianity has been reduced to just one more voice competing for attention in the market-place of ideas. Failing to recognize how much it owes to the Christian tradition, our culture has increasingly cast aside many of the positive elements that made it what it is. Perhaps, though, the fact that Christianity is no longer the central belief system of our culture gives us the opportunity to speak in clearer and more powerful ways, as it is not so easy to confuse the Christian faith with our modern cultural religion. As "cultural religiosity" falters in its impact on twenty-first-century-people, the radical imperatives of the gospel of grace can perhaps penetrate the religious veneer of the Western world and strike deeply into our hearts. Certainly a number of writers of great skill and insight have taken up this challenge.

G. K. CHESTERTON (1874-1936)
Orthodoxy
The Everlasting Man
The Man Who Was Thursday
Father Brown stories

"The Shakespeare of the aphorism" is the title that someone has given to Gilbert Keith Chesterton. He had the ability to pack more paradox and more truth into a single sentence than possibly any writer in history. This characteristic makes his books a joy to read for their penetrating insight and their infectious cleverness. Put this together with a swashbuckling faith, a warm and joyous sense of humor, and a dependence on plain common sense, and you have a fine definition of Chesterton's highly individual gift. It is a tough call to say which is better: his highly original nonfiction (for example, *Orthodoxy, The Everlasting Man*) or his always-entertaining fiction (for example, the Father Brown stories and *The Man Who Was Thursday*). Read both for a model of a man who enjoyed his faith.

> Because children have abounding vitality, because they are in spirit fierce and free, therefore they want things repeated and unchanged. They always say, "Do it again"; and the grown-up person does it again until he is nearly dead. For grown-up people are not strong enough to exult in monotony. It is possible that God says every morning, "Do it again" to the sun; and every evening, "Do it again" to the moon. It may not be automatic necessity that makes all daisies alike; it may be that God makes every daisy separately, but has never got tired of making them. It may be that He has the eternal appetite of infancy; for we have sinned and grown old, and our Father is younger than we. The repetition in Nature may not be a mere recurrence; it may be a theatrical encore.
>
> G. K. CHESTERTON, *Orthodoxy*

EVELYN UNDERHILL (1875-1941)
Mysticism

The definitive study of mysticism and its manifestations, written with great sympathy by a woman who was herself a mystic of note. This is the book to begin with if you wish to study the phenomenon of mysticism.

JOHN GRESHAM MACHEN (1881-1937)
Christianity and Liberalism

A fearless defender of orthodox Christianity in a time when it appeared that theological liberalism would take the day, Machen had a fiery passion tempered by an exceedingly astute mind and a generosity of spirit. Those who call themselves theological conservatives owe him a great debt of gratitude for his clarion call to the church in the early part of the twentieth century.

PIERRE TEILHARD DE CHARDIN (1881-1955)
The Phenomenon of Man
The Divine Milieu

Teilhard was a French priest with an expertise in paleontology who tried to combine the key tenets of evolutionary theory with the teachings of the church. Although he was officially censured and silenced by the church, his mystical vision of cosmic spiritual evolution has continued to be very influential. Whatever conclusion you draw about his orthodoxy, his writings are both highly original and intriguing. For some, he is one of the greatest of modern mystics; to others, a heretical forerunner to modern "cosmic consciousness" and New Age thinking. Either way, his influence is undeniable.

JACQUES MARITAIN (1882-1973)
True Humanism

One of the key works of this French philosopher, this book attempts to demonstrate that Christianity is the truest form of humanism. Maritain is never easy to read, but there is much insight to be drawn from his dense philosophical prose.

RUDOLF BULTMANN (1884-1976)
Jesus Christ and Mythology

Bultmann is known best for his project of "demythologization"—the stripping of the Gospel accounts of all their mythic and supernatural content in the attempt to reach the core teachings of Jesus. Whether this is a powerful tool for making the gospel relevant to today's scientific mindset or just another form of reductionism (my opinion) is for the reader to decide. C. S. Lewis might have said that Bultmann suffers from "chronological snobbery"—the tendency to judge the old in the light of the new. Whatever conclusion you draw about his orthodoxy, his work has had a huge influence on the way much of theology is approached in our century.

FRANÇOIS MAURIAC (1885-1970)
Thérèse Desqueyroux
Viper's Tangle

Searing, introspective novels about sin and grace by the award-winning

French writer, these works far transcend the category of general religious fiction. Mauriac uses the realities of the human condition as the springboard for his profound theological musings in fictional form.

KARL BARTH (1886-1968)
Church Dogmatics
The Word of God and the Word of Man

One of the major names in contemporary theology, Barth produced a shelf full of books on theological matters, including his multivolume *Church Dogmatics*. Barth founded his theology on the revelation of God in Jesus Christ. His writing is very learned and based on careful exegesis of Scripture, yet it has a freshness that makes his basic orthodoxy seem somehow unique and original. Geoffrey Bromiley has attempted to summarize Barth's ideas in *An Introduction to Karl Barth*. Bernard Ramm's study of Barth, *After Fundamentalism*, will be of special interest to evangelicals.

> Human thoughts about God do not constitute the content of the Bible; rather, it is the true divine thought about humanity. The Bible does not tell us how we should speak about God but what God says to us, not how we may find the way to him but how he has sought and found the way to us, not what is the proper relation in which we must stand to him but what is the covenant that he has made with all who in faith are the children of Abraham, and that he has sealed once and for all in Jesus Christ. This is what stands in the Bible.
>
> KARL BARTH, *The Word of God and the Word of Man*

CHARLES WILLIAMS (1886-1945)
Descent into Hell
The Place of the Lion

A colleague and friend of C. S. Lewis and J. R. R. Tolkien, Williams produced a series of highly unusual novels characterized by their preoccupation with the inbreaking of the supernatural dimension into our world. They are filled with bizarre occurrences, moments of numinous revelation and the depiction of intense spiritual experiences. Readers will find him either repellingly strange or, as I do, utterly fascinating.

PAUL TILLICH (1886-1965)

The Courage to Be

Written by a controversial liberal theologian who was a great thinker and communicator, this book perhaps shows Tillich at his best, trying to communicate the gospel to the thoroughly modern individual. Even those who cannot agree with his theology will find his work full of insight and reflection.

T. S. ELIOT (1888-1965)

The Waste Land
"Ash Wednesday"
The Four Quartets
The Family Reunion
The Cocktail Party
Murder in the Cathedral

The finest modern poet and also a committed believer, T. S. Eliot captured so well the hopelessness of life without faith and the mysterious power of faith to transform lives and give meaning to human experience. I personally count reading *Four Quartets* among the most powerful spiritual experiences of my life. It is an almost inexhaustible source of profound meditation on time and eternity and their intersection in the present moment. Eliot is not always easy to read, but he is unquestionably worth the effort. His plays (including *The Family Reunion, The Cocktail Party, Murder in the Cathedral*) are profound musings on themes of guilt and grace, with deep theological underpinnings.

> Who is the third who walks always beside you?
> When I count, there are only you and I together
> But when I look ahead up the white road
> There is always another one walking beside you
> Gliding wrapt in a brown mantle, hooded
> I do not know whether a man or a woman
> —But who is that on the other side of you? T. S. ELIOT, *The Waste Land*

GEORGES BERNANOS (1888-1948)
Diary of a Country Priest

A simple but beautiful tale of doubt, faith and self-sacrifice. Bernanos's hero is a young priest whose life is riddled with self-doubt and questioning, but who nevertheless provides those around him with a powerful witness to the love and mercy of God. Some of the passages in this book are truly heart wrenching.

GABRIEL MARCEL (1889-1973)
The Mystery of Being

The major work by this French Catholic philosopher, Marcel agrees with modern existentialism that human existence is hard to make sense of, but emphasizes the difference between "life as a problem" (the view of most moderns) and "life as a mystery" (the Christian perspective). He criticizes Sartre's atheistic existentialism for its abstraction and its distance from the actual lives of human being. Difficult, but worth the effort.

BORIS PASTERNAK (1890-1960)
Doctor Zhivago

This powerful novel contains many Christian elements that are missing from the classic movie of the same name. Pasternak had a poet's touch in his descriptions of mood and place.

J. R. R. TOLKIEN (1892-1973)
The Hobbit
The Lord of the Rings trilogy

The immensely popular works of Tolkien can be read on two levels: (1) as very exciting and moving adventure tales or (2) as a personal mythology that is deeply indebted to Norse mythology, Arthurian legend and the Christian gospel. These are gripping tales of heroism, loyalty, courage and sacrifice. But even more, they are a strong testimony to the providence of God and the hope of the ultimate triumph of good over evil. To better understand their religious underpinnings, read Tolkien's more difficult (but very rewarding) epic, *The Silmarillion,* and the fine biography by Humphrey Carpenter.

REINHOLD NIEBUHR (1892-1971)

Leaves from the Notebook of a Tamed Cynic
Moral Man and Immoral Society
The Nature and Destiny of Man

One of the most important American theologians, Niebuhr combined a deep passion for social justice, a strong grasp of intellectual history and a profound sense of human sinfulness and finiteness. His writing is lively and honest enough that in his own time it gained him many readers, even among those who could not accept his theology.

THOMAS KELLY (1893-1941)

A Testament of Devotion

From the Quaker tradition, Kelly delivers a call for simplicity, inner silence and the necessity for attuning one's heart and spirit to the voice of God. This book deserves a slow and meditative reading.

DOROTHY L. SAYERS (1893-1957)

The Man Born to Be King
The Mind of the Maker
Christian Letters to a Post-Christian World
Creed or Chaos

The author of the popular Lord Peter Wimsey detective novels was also the writer of wonderful religious dramas (*The Man Born to Be King* is a magnificent play covering the life of Christ) and witty apologetic writings. Sayers stressed the parallel between the image of God as seen in human creativity and the creativity of the Creator. She was firmly convinced of the reasonableness of orthodox Christianity and was one of its most able modern defenders.

H. RICHARD NIEBUHR (1894-1962)

Christ and Culture

A very suggestive and important study of the different models that Christians tend to use to relate their faith to culture. Absolutely essential reading for anyone interested in the question of how we can integrate our faith with the modern world.

A. W. TOZER (1897-1963)

The Pursuit of God

Tozer manages to break out of the cliché-ridden lingo that characterizes much of the evangelical writing on the spiritual life. What emerges is a book notable for its depth of insight into the human spirit and for the single-hearted passion of its author for the Savior. Magnificent!

> To have found God and still to pursue Him is the soul's paradox of love, scorned indeed by the too-easily-satisfied religionist, but justified in happy experience by the children of the burning heart.
>
> Come near to the holy men and women of the past and you will soon feel the heat of their desire after God. They mourned for Him, they prayed and wrestled and sought for Him day and night, in season and out, and when they had found Him the finding was all the sweeter for the long seeking. A. W. TOZER, *The Pursuit of God*

C. S. LEWIS (1898-1963)

Mere Christianity
The Screwtape Letters
The Great Divorce
The Abolition of Man
Till We Have Faces
The Weight of Glory and Other Addresses
Chronicles of Narnia
The Space trilogy

Perhaps no other writer of the twentieth century has done more for the cause of orthodox Christian faith than Clive Staples Lewis. His combination of a vigorous commitment to the reasonableness of faith and his soaring creativity produced a body of work that gives hope to the modern person who finds so many modern pronouncements of faith to be sterile and mindless. For me personally, his work is a veritable lifeline thrown into a Christian subculture that is so often intellectually and creatively stagnant. By all means do not miss reading Lewis, and don't stop with the list above. These titles are just a sample of the rewarding reading experiences Lewis offers. If you are interested in an in-depth look at Lewis's life and teaching, you might want to read my book *Not a Tame*

Lion: The Spiritual Legacy of C. S. Lewis.

> At present we are on the outside of the world, the wrong side of the door. We discern the freshness and purity of morning, but they do not make us fresh and pure. We cannot mingle with the splendours we see. But all the leaves of the New Testament are rustling with the rumour that it will not always be so. Some day, God willing, we shall get in.
>
> It is a serious thing to live in a society of possible gods and goddesses, to remember that the dullest and most uninteresting person you talk to may one day be a creature which, if you saw it now, you would be strongly tempted to worship, or else a horror and corruption such as you now meet, if at all, only in a nightmare. All day long we are, in some degree, helping each other to one or other of these destinations. It is in the light of these overwhelming possibilities, it is with the awe and circumspection proper to them, that we should conduct all our dealings with one another, all friendships, all loves, all play, all politics. There are no ordinary people. C. S. LEWIS, "The Weight of Glory"

IGNAZIO SILONE (1900-1978)
Bread and Wine

An excellent novel by an Italian Catholic writer who struggles with the relationship of faith and politics in fascist Italy during the years surrounding World War II. It is the story of an unbeliever, disguised as a priest to avoid persecution, who finds his life and attitudes slowly changing. Silone's insights into politics and faith make this an important and fascinating read.

EVELYN WAUGH (1903-1966)
A Handful of Dust
Brideshead Revisited

A deft comic touch marks all the work of this important British novelist. His constant theme is the vacuity of life without God. Rather than concentrating on the joys of faith, this talented curmudgeon emphasizes the boredom and stifling meaninglessness of a life that is focused on this world's attractions. His work offers both a powerful critique of modern aimlessness and tremendous entertainment. These two novels are marked by beautiful writing, wry humor and a painfully accurate depiction of the desperateness of the human condition.

MALCOLM MUGGERIDGE (1903-1990)
Jesus Rediscovered
The End of Christendom
Something Beautiful for God

Muggeridge was a British journalist who, late in life, became a convert to Catholicism. He is in many ways the archetypical curmudgeon: skeptical, cranky and dryly humorous. But his best work also evidences an unexpected tenderness and passion. He was a fearless defender of Christian truth and a writer of amazing clarity and style. His book *The Third Testament* reveals those who influenced him the most: Kierkegaard, Pascal, Blake and Dostoyevsky, among others. To say that he is worthy company for these great thinkers and authors is to give an idea of his own talent and originality.

GRAHAM GREENE (1904-1991)
The Power and the Glory
The Heart of the Matter
The End of the Affair
Monsignor Quixote

Greene is almost universally acknowledged as one of the great novelists of the twentieth century. His books often center on spiritual themes which he unfolds with insight, suspense and authenticity. Many of Greene's books observe human beings attempting to hold on to some shred of faith in an extremely dark situation. His works testify to the difficulty of the life of faith and trumpet the virtues of loyalty and courage. Most of his books demonstrate his unusual ability to create not only vivid characters but also to produce an unforgettable atmosphere wherein the story unfolds (some have jokingly referred to it as "Greeneland"). His best-known work is probably *The Power and the Glory,* about an alcoholic priest on the run in Mexico at a time when Christianity is outlawed and all priests are being systematically eliminated. Pursued by an upright law officer who is an atheist, the priest struggles against his own faltering faith and the unrelenting pursuit of the police. The priest's heroic demise is testimony to the strength of the gospel, even in the face of our flaws. *Monsignor Quixote* is a lighter and funnier but equally evocative tale.

DIETRICH BONHOEFFER (1906-1945)
The Cost of Discipleship
Life Together
Letters and Papers from Prison

Bonhoeffer has been interpreted in many differing ways by people from every part of the theological spectrum. The one thing that is indisputable is that he was a gifted and original thinker and a courageous human being. At a time when many in Germany made concessions to the Nazi regime, Bonhoeffer stood strong and true for the integrity of the gospel. He worked to thwart the plans of Hitler and to strengthen the underground church. When he was offered safety in America, he chose to return to Germany and continue his work against Nazi oppression. He was sent to a concentration camp and, just a few days before it was liberated by the Allies, he was executed. Many of his ideas are critical to the modern theological dialogue: "the world come of age," "religionless Christianity," "cheap grace" and "costly grace," to name a few. He causes us to think deeply about what it means to live as a Christian in the modern world. Here was a man of passion, conviction and gentle spirituality whose life story is as inspiring as his work.

The Cost of Discipleship is a study of the meaning of true grace and a reflection on the Sermon on the Mount. *Life Together* is a rich study of the spiritual life and community. It is full of wise advice on growing spiritually. *Letters and Papers from Prison* is a collection of his last writings and the profound reflections on life and faith that occupied his mind during his last days. The biography by Eberhard Bethge is a classic study by a close friend.

> Cheap grace is the preaching of forgiveness without requiring repentance, baptism without church discipline, communion without confession, absolution without personal confession. Cheap grace is grace without discipleship, grace without the cross, grace without Jesus Christ, living and incarnate.
>
> Costly grace is costly because it calls us to follow, and it is grace because it

calls us to follow Jesus Christ. It is costly because it costs a man his life, and it is grace because it gives a man the only true life. It is costly because it condemns sin, and grace because it justifies the sinner. Above all, it is costly because it cost God the life of his Son. DIETRICH BONHOEFFER, *The Cost of Discipleship*

W. H. AUDEN (1907-1973)
Poems

A thoroughly modern poet, Auden believed that only the Christian faith holds the real truth about our lives. He wrote powerful poems on many topics (and was a fine essayist as well) and had the ability to create phrases that remain in the consciousness long after his books have been returned to the shelf.

HELMUT THIELICKE (1908-1985)
The Waiting Father
Theological Ethics

Thielicke deserves to be much better known among American evangelicals than he is. He was a German theologian who had that rarest of gifts: the ability to communicate orthodoxy in a way that is intellectually satisfying and yet takes into account the difficult hurdles that the modern skeptic must overcome to believe. His wide-ranging intellect, demonstrated over the entirety of his work, is staggering. He seems to have read and reflected on nearly everything of importance, and his conclusions are both orthodox and fresh at the same time. His talent for delivering sermons made him a hero in postwar Germany, where people flocked to hear the gospel preached by this courageous and talented man.

The Waiting Father demonstrates his gift as a preacher and expositor as he reflects on the parable of the prodigal son. His insights will astound and inspire you. *Theological Ethics* is one of his scholarly works and evidences careful thinking, exhaustive research and spiritual depth.

SIMONE WEIL (1909-1943)
Waiting for God

A spiritual pilgrim who was never able to feel comfortable in the established church, Weil identified with the needs and experiences of the common person and gave her life in a quiet heroism to that end. She died at a young age following her heroic efforts during World War II. Weil was a social activist, a scholar and a writer of unusual ability. *Waiting for God* contains her spiritual reflections. Robert Coles, something of a kindred spirit to Weil, has written an insightful biography.

FRANCIS SCHAEFFER (1912-1984)
The God Who Is There
How Should We Then Live?

When Francis Schaeffer's first works were published in the late 1960s, his was a voice that the evangelical church needed to hear. He called for intellectual respectability, artistic integrity and authentic Christian living. Time has shown that his insights were truly prophetic. He foresaw much of what was coming in terms of the growth of secularism and moral decay. Schaeffer desired to reach a mass audience with a philosophical message about the meaning of life and the truth of the Christian faith. Few have been so successful in this difficult goal. Schaeffer especially deserves applause for his encouragement of the arts and culture in the often anti-art evangelical subculture. The basic outlines of his thought are best captured in his "trilogy" *(The God Who Is There, Escape from Reason* and *He Is There and He Is Not Silent)* and illustrated in his survey of modern history *(How Should We Then Live?).*

THOMAS MERTON (1915-1968)
The Seven Storey Mountain
New Seeds of Contemplation
Thoughts in Solitude

A Trappist monk and devotional writer of great depth and wide appeal, Merton crystallizes the experience of the modern Christian for many of his admiring readers. His best work arises out of his own concerns and struggles. Here is a modern odyssey of the spirit wedded with a writing ability that could have made him a considerable novelist. His work is richly contemplative.

Several fine biographies exist about this major influence on modern spiritual life: Michael Mott's *The Seven Mountains of Thomas Merton,* Monica

Furlong's *Thomas Merton* and William H. Shannon's *Silent Lamp* (my favorite). All deal with the difficult question of Merton's flirtation late in life with Eastern thought.

> My Lord God, I have no idea where I am going. I do not see the road ahead of me. I cannot know for certain where it will end. Nor do I really know myself, and the fact that I think I am following your will does not mean I am actually doing so. But I believe that the desire to please you does in fact please you. And I hope I have that desire in all that I am doing. I hope that if I do this you will lead me by the right road, though I may know nothing about it. Therefore I will trust you always though I may seem to be lost and in the shadow of death. I will not fear, for you are ever with me, and you will never leave me to face my perils alone.
> THOMAS MERTON, *Thoughts in Solitude*

FLANNERY O'CONNOR (1925-1964)
Wise Blood
Mystery and Manners
A Good Man Is Hard to Find
Everything That Rises Must Converge

O'Connor, a leading Southern author who was an unabashed believer, wrote wonderfully strange short stories and novels. Many will find O'Connor's stories perplexing until they understand what she was trying to do: to shock the reader into a realization of his or her own sinfulness and self-deceit. *Mystery and Manners* is a collection of essays that discuss her Christian perspective on art and writing. Her unusual and unforgettable stories are not to be missed; they will haunt your imagination long after you finish reading them.

MARTIN LUTHER KING JR. (1929-1968)
Strength to Love

Besides being one of the most potent political figures of the twentieth century, Martin Luther King Jr. was an inspired orator; this collection of writings captures his prophetic voice very well. Even a cursory perusal of his sermons will reveal the consistent presence of biblical imagery in his writings and orations. King's model was the prophetic tradition of the Old Testament, and his own thundering rhetoric is similarly filled with indignation, the promise of judgment and prophecy of the coming reign of righteousness.

A One-Year Plan for Exploring the Classics

If you are interested in beginning to explore the classic books of our Christian heritage (discussed in this chapter), one of the hurdles you might face is knowing where to begin. With that in mind, I have created a one-year plan of suggested readings that will allow you to sample some of the very best in Christian writing: books on spirituality, theology, autobiography, novels, even poetry. I've chosen these books from a variety of historical periods so you get a sense of the continuity throughout time and the uniqueness of each era. If you commit yourself to this schedule for one year (this still leaves plenty of room for reading other books), you'll be on your way to a deeper appreciation for the rich variety and profound quality of the Christian tradition.

Richard Foster has written two books that provide a general orientation to the classics.

Celebration of Discipline (an excellent overview of the spiritual disciplines)

Devotional Classics (a sampling from the classics)

These books would make for a good introduction before you set out on your year-long adventure.

January: Augustine

The Confessions [Books 1-10] (the first and still greatest spiritual autobiography)

February: John Bunyan

Pilgrim's Progress (a fictional parable of the spiritual journey)

March: Blaise Pascal

Pensées (a compelling argument for the truth of Christianity that speaks to both heart and mind)

April: Thomas à Kempis and Brother Lawrence

Thomas à Kempis, *The Imitation of Christ* (the classic book on spiritiual living)

Brother Lawrence, *The Practice of the Presence of God* (a life-changing look at prayer as a way of life)

May: Teresa of Ávila

Teresa of Ávila, *Interior Castle* (one of the most balanced of Christian mystics)

(Extra credit: read some of the work of John of the Cross, a contemporary of Teresa)

June: Fyodor Dostoyevsky

Fyodor Dostoyevsky, *The Brothers Karamazov* (arguably the greatest novel ever written, and one with profound spiritual content)

July: The Great Theologians

Explore the work of the great formulators of faith.
Sample excerpts from the following:

   Thomas Aquinas, *Summa Theologica* (Pt. 1, Questions 1-26)
   Martin Luther, "On Christian Liberty"
   John Calvin, *Institutes of the Christian Religion* (Bk. 1)
   John Wesley, *The Journals of John Wesley*

August: Dietrich Bonhoeffer

The Cost of Discipleship (especially Part One, "Grace and Discipleship," a World War II-era call to sacrificial commitment)
Life Together (the place of solitude and community in the Christian faith)

September: Christian Poetry

Experience the beauty and power of Christian lyric.
William Blake, *Songs of Innocence and of Experience*
John Donne, *Holy Sonnets*
T. S. Eliot, "Ash Wednesday" and *Four Quartets*
George Herbert, selected poems
Gerard Manley Hopkins, selected poems

October: G. K. Chesterton

The Man Who Was Thursday (a strange and fascinating parable of faith)
Orthodoxy (a humorous and convincing argument for faith)

November: C. S. Lewis

Mere Christianity (unsurpassed discussion of the basics of faith)
The Lion, the Witch, and the Wardrobe (a children's book for all ages)

December: A. W. Tozer and Henri Nouwen

These two authors are nearly our contemporaries.

Henri Nouwen, *The Way of the Heart* (exploration of the lessons Nouwen learned from the ancient desert fathers)

A. W. Tozer, *The Pursuit of God* (a challenge to serious faith)

FOUR

OTHER CLASSIC WRITINGS

We have already explored some of the great writing that has arisen out of the Christian tradition. But there is also a great body of literature by those who came too early in time to be influenced by Christianity, by those who were only marginally influenced by it and even by those who were actively hostile toward faith. Their books, though founded on other worldviews, nonetheless have a great deal to say to the discerning Christian reader. First, because as sharers in our common human experience they can provide valuable insights about living; second, because all human beings can draw on the richness of God's general revelation; and third, because sometimes those outside our tradition can see our faults and failures more clearly than we can from inside that tradition.

If you are interested in a fuller theological justification for reading books by those outside the Christian tradition, see appendix B, "Plundering the Egyptians."

The Ancient World

It is to our own detriment that modern Christians are, in general, unfamiliar with the great classics of Greece and Rome. It is clear that the apostle Paul was an attentive student of these books and used them to aid in the proclamation of the gospel (see Acts 17:28). The ancient writers were close observers of humanity who help us better understand ourselves and the need for human beings to live ethically and with dignity.

HOMER (CA. 850 B.C.)

The Iliad
The Odyssey

How can one over-praise Homer, the fountainhead of Western literature? When read in a good translation (like Richmond Lattimore's *The Iliad*, Robert Fitzgerald's *The Odyssey* or the fine translations of Robert Fagles), these are works of intense beauty and riveting action, full of memorable incidents and characters and truly heroic (if flawed) examples of virtue and character.

> Sing in me, Muse, and through me tell the story
> of that man skilled in all ways of contending,
> the wanderer, harried for years on end,
> after he plundered the stronghold
> on the proud height of Troy. HOMER, *The Odyssey*

AESCHYLUS (525-456 B.C.)

The Orestia
Prometheus Bound

The Orestia is a difficult but powerful trilogy of plays about revenge, guilt and atonement from the first of the great Greek dramatists. I recommend the translation by Richmond Lattimore. *Prometheus Bound* is a mythic drama about human limitation in the face of the power of the gods.

SOPHOCLES (CA. 496-406 B.C.)

Oedipus the King
Antigone
Philoctetes

Oedipus is, of course, the best-known drama of the Greek playwrights—and rightfully so. Playwrights, novelists, philosophers and psychologists have all explored its rich and evocative themes. It is truly one of the most important works of our culture, but the other plays by Sophocles are also worthy of attention.

ARISTOPHANES (CA. 448-380 B.C.)
The Clouds
The Frogs
The Birds
Lysistrata

The witty and bawdy humor of Aristophanes still holds up well after all these centuries. The targets of his wit remain current: philosophy and the academic life *(The Clouds)*, literature and drama *(The Frogs)*, sex and male-female relationships *(Lysistrata)* and politics *(The Birds)*. His comedies are at the same time vulgar and lyrical. One must read him to understand how this is possible.

EURIPIDES (CA. 484-406 B.C.)
Trojan Women
The Bacchae

The last of the great Athenian dramatists, Euripides' work is marked by its unwavering cynicism. In this and other ways he is much closer to the modern temper than the older Greek dramatists.

PLATO (CA. 428-348 B.C.)
The Symposium
The Republic
Last Dialogues of Socrates

One modern philosopher has written that all the history of philosophy is merely a footnote to Plato. The measure of Plato's greatness is that this is hardly an overstatement. The profundity of his work has left an indelible mark on the way we live and think. Christian philosophers through the ages have found much in Plato to illuminate the human experience and our relationship to the divine. Recently the work of Eric Voegelin has used Plato's thought as a guide to the complexities of history and existence. For both depth of wisdom and pure entertainment (the dialogues are both utterly convincing and sometimes wryly humorous), the work of Plato deserves close reading by Christians.

> Until philosophers are kings, or the kings and princes of the world have the spirit and power of philosophy, and political greatness and wisdom meet in one, and those commoner natures who pursue either to the exclusion of the other are compelled to stand aside, cities will never have rest from their evils—no, nor the human race, as I believe—and then only will this our State have a possibility of life and behold the light of day. PLATO, *The Republic*

ARISTOTLE (384-322 B.C.)
Nicomachean Ethics
Poetics

For the sheer magnitude of the subjects that Aristotle (Plato's student and teacher of Alexander the Great) covered in his many writings, there is no comparison. His knowledge was encyclopedic, and his logic was careful and usually persuasive. Aristotle set the terms for most of the ongoing theological and philosophical disputes that raged from the Middle Ages on, making him, along with Plato, one of the twin pillars upon which Western thought is founded. A valuable introduction to his thought for the beginning reader of Aristotle is Mortimer J. Adler's *Aristotle for Everybody*.

> For the man who flies from and fears everything and does not stand his ground against anything becomes a coward, and the man who fears nothing at all but goes to meet every danger becomes rash; and similarly the man who indulges in every pleasure and abstains from none becomes self-indulgent, while the man who shuns every pleasure, as boors do, becomes in a way insensible; temperance and courage, then are destroyed by excess and defect, and preserved by the mean. ARISTOTLE, *Nicomachean Ethics*

LUCRETIUS (CA. 95-55 B.C.)
On the Nature of Things

This poetic philosophical musing by the first great materialist philosopher, and an early Western proponent of atheism, anticipated many of the prejudices of modern secularism centuries before their rise.

VIRGIL (70-19 B.C.)
The Aeneid

Virgil's epic is matched in scope and brilliance only by the work of Homer, his great model. This powerful poem deals with events following the fall of Troy and the founding of the Roman Empire. A stately and often tragic work, the translation by Robert Fitzgerald is particularly good.

MARCUS AURELIUS (121-180)
Meditations

A Roman emperor and stoic philosopher, Aurelius meditates on the vicissitudes of human existence and on how to live in peace and serenity in the midst of a chaotic world. A work of beauty and depth, whose influence stretches down to our own time.

> Let thy chief fort and place of defense be, a mind free from passions. A stronger place and better fortified than this, hath no man.
> MARCUS AURELIUS, *Meditations*

PLOTINUS (205-270)
Enneads

Highly influential to the mystical tradition, Plotinus takes the Platonic theories a step further in his teachings, emphasizing the release of the soul from the prison of the body. Some extreme forms of medieval mysticism unfortunately tried to incorporate these ideas into Christianity and produced a faith that deprecates the human experience and the joy of the created order. We still reap the fruit of his rejection of the earthly sphere in some religious forms of extreme self-denial.

The Middle Ages

The Middle Ages most definitely show the stamp of a predominantly Christian culture. This was a time when just about everything in the Western world revolved around the Christian vision of reality (though often imperfectly lived out)—even for those writers at the fringes of the Christian worldview. But changes were brewing that would eventually bring secularism into ascendancy.

SNORRI STURLUSON (1179-1241)
Prose Edda

This is the classic source for much of Norse mythology: Odin, Thor, the battles of the gods and the final apocalyptic war, Ragnarok. These tales of violence and valor have provided the themes for much of the great art of European culture. Christians will find it interesting to note how Sturluson, in the early chapters of this work, attempts to connect this mythology with biblical stories.

UNKNOWN
Beowulf

A heroic narrative poem from the early Anglo-Saxon tradition about the battle of Beowulf against a dragon. Many astute readers will note the subtle, but undoubtedly purposeful, analogies to the Gospels.

PETRARCH (1304-1374)
Sonnets
Ascent of Mt. Ventoux

This author of romantic lyrical love poems, and a key figure in our modern conception of romance, was a founder of Renaissance humanism. His *Ascent of Mt. Ventoux* in some ways parallels Augustine's *Confessions*. It provides an interesting comparison to the conversion of Augustine, as a similar experience nets different results.

GIOVANNI BOCCACCIO (1313-1375)
The Decameron

A collection of tales about love, romance, sex, unfaithfulness and deception, this book is frequently uproariously funny, often in bad taste, nearly always entertaining.

The Early Modern World

The Renaissance was a rebirth of classical civilization, a revaluation of the dignity of the individual human being and the creation of a new openness to intellectual inquiry. Breaking free from the bonds of tradition gave a new impulse to the arts and sciences, but it also planted the seeds of a new worldview, one that pushed God and religion toward the periphery of intellectual concern. Some thinkers stressed human autonomy to such a degree that the importance of faith was greatly diminished.

LEONARDO DA VINCI (1452-1519)
Notebooks

These notebooks of one of the greatest Renaissance painters show a man of incredible intelligence and creativity, and an inventor of astonishing fertility. It is to him that the term "Renaissance man" most fully refers.

MACHIAVELLI (1469-1527)
The Prince

In this guide for those in places of leadership, Machiavelli shows the truth of the old motto: The more things change, the more they stay the same. His advice is mercenary and tyrannical, but from a historical perspective it has proven frighteningly effective.

RABELAIS (CA. 1483-1553)
Gargantua and Pantagruel

A long, witty work that is a strange mixture of fantasy, satire and bawdy humor. It is notable for its rich language and odd plot twists. By all means, try to locate the poetical translation by Sir Thomas Urquart and Peter Motteux, which so well captures the marvelously playful way that Rabelais used words.

MICHEL DE MONTAIGNE (1533-1592)
Essays

One of the great prose stylists of all time, Montaigne's wise and witty essays range over almost every conceivable subject. He boldly puts forth himself, his own personality, as the main subject of his work. Montaigne strove to ask questions that penetrate beyond appearances and challenge our perceptions: "When I play with my cat who knows if she does not amuse herself more with me than I with her?" T. S. Eliot said of him that he gives voice to the skepticism in every human heart, and many credit him as one of the founders of relativism.

> Each man calls barbarism whatever is not his own practice; for indeed it seems we have no other test of truth than the example and pattern of the opinions and customs of the country we live in. MICHEL DE MONTAIGNE, *Essays*

MIGUEL DE CERVANTES (1547-1616)
Don Quixote

A humorous, and often very touching, novel about the adventures of a knight-errant and his sidekick, Sancho Panza. Full of invention, funny scenes and clever conversations, this book takes aim at the excesses of the romantic literature of the time. Because of Cervantes's tendency to stray far from the story at hand and to pen some fairly tiresome poetry, *Don Quixote* is one of the few classics I would recommend reading in an abridgment.

FRANCIS BACON (1561-1626)
Essays
The New Atlantis

Thought-provoking essays and futuristic thinking by the early English philosopher who coined the phrase "knowledge is power."

THOMAS HOBBES (1588-1679)
Leviathan

Not a Sunday-afternoon-at-the-beach read but a very influential book. Hobbes was an English political philosopher whose religious skepticism was ahead of its time.

RENÉ DESCARTES (1596-1650)
Discourse on Method

This French philosopher, originator of the famous dictum "I think, therefore I am," taught that certainty came from intuition and deduction, and emphasized the split between mind and matter. One of the aims of Pascal's *Pensees* was to refute Descartes's self-assured conclusions.

MOLIÈRE (1622-1673)
The Imaginary Invalid
The Misanthrope
Tartuffe
The School for Wives

These hilarious dramas built around class, gender and social foibles hold up well in our modern times. The clever dialogue, frenetic plot twists and humorous characterizations make Molière a delight to read. Richard Wilbur's excellent translations capture well the marvelous humor of this talented comic playwright.

BENEDICT DE SPINOZA (1632-1677)
Ethics

This is the major work of this influential Jewish pantheistic philosopher, whose thought is marked by logical argumentation and a humane tolerance.

JOHN LOCKE (1632-1704)
An Essay Concerning Human Understanding

One of the key modern works in philosophy, this essay focuses on a question of epistemology, How can we know? Locke was famous for the idea of the *tabula rasa* (the blank slate). This book is not an easy read, but it is full of important and influential ideas.

The Eighteenth Century

The Enlightenment was a time of the exchange of certainties. No longer was religion seen to have the undisputable answers to human questionings. Enlightenment thinkers instead saw reason as the final court of appeal in the quest for understanding. This period was one marked by a great confidence in humankind's ability to solve its own problems and create a better world through the use of reason. But the failure of many of these thinkers to fully reckon with the reality of human fallenness opened the door to the excesses and cruelties of the coming age of revolutions. The eventual decline of confidence in the power of reason left humankind searching but not finding.

VOLTAIRE (1694-1778)
Candide

Voltaire epitomizes the Enlightenment for many readers. His trust in reason seems unquenchable, but he saw clearly the foibles of human beings and their addiction to superstitions. His writing is lively, immensely enjoyable and provides much food for thought, even if his thinking is not always satisfying. Parts of *Candide* will leave you laughing out loud.

If God did not exist it would be necessary to invent Him.

Prejudices are what fools use for reason.

Man is not born wicked; he becomes so in the same way as he becomes sick.

Of all religions, Christianity is without doubt the one that should inspire tolerance most, although, up to now, the Christians have been the most intolerant of all men. VOLTAIRE, various aphorisms

HENRY FIELDING (1707-1754)
Tom Jones

Tom Jones is a rowdy and ribald coming-of-age novel, full of incident and adventure. One of the great early masterpieces of English literature.

DAVID HUME (1711-1776)
An Enquiry Concerning Human Understanding

A British philosopher of empiricism, Hume's ideas have had a major effect on modern thinking.

JEAN JACQUES ROUSSEAU (1712-1778)
Confessions
The Social Contract

To say that Rousseau, the great predecessor of the Romantics, was modern before his time is not necessarily a compliment, for he represents much that is unfortunate in modern beliefs and attitudes: an egotistical preoccupation with self, a disregard for authority and tradition, and an unrealistically utopian view of human nature. He is, however, a writer of clarity and interest, whose influence on our modern ways of thinking probably cannot be exaggerated.

Man is born free, and everywhere he is in chains.

By equality, we should understand, not that the degrees of power and riches are to be absolutely identical for everybody; but that power shall never be so strong as to be capable of violence and shall always be exercised by virtue of rank and law; and that, in respect to riches, no citizen shall ever be wealthy enough to buy another, and none poor enough to be forced to sell himself.
JEAN JACQUES ROUSSEAU, *The Social Contract*

LAURENCE STERNE (1713-1768)
Tristram Shandy

In this strange and experimental novel, Sterne uses many techniques that predate the style of a number of important modern writers. It is also, at points, quite funny!

ADAM SMITH (1723-1790)
The Wealth of Nations

This book is the classic defense of capitalism and the "hidden hand" that makes it function. Highly influential in the development of modern economic thought.

IMMANUEL KANT (1724-1804)
The Critique of Pure Reason

This volume is an extremely difficult philosophical exploration of the nature of human reason. If you can't make sense of this dense prose—and you are not alone if you can't—you might want first to read about Kant in a good history of philosophy. (I can recommend no better such history than that of Catholic scholar Frederick Copleston, now available in three lengthy paperback volumes.)

THOMAS PAINE (1737-1809)
The Rights of Man

An important document in the American call for independence, and a searing indictment of tyranny and injustice.

EDWARD GIBBON (1737-1794)
Decline and Fall of the Roman Empire

In Gibbon's famous study of the causes for the fall of the Roman Empire, Christianity is unfairly criticized as the major culprit. Most modern historians would dispute a good deal of his argument, but it remains, nonetheless, an influential work for its style and the expansiveness of its thinking.

JAMES BOSWELL (1740-1795)
The Life of Samuel Johnson

This biography of one of the greatest men of letters is full of insight, humor and entertaining anecdote.

JAMES MADISON (1751-1836) AND OTHERS
The Federalist Papers

A collection of documents containing the debates that raged during our nation's birth about how to construct a truly free and just government. In these pages you'll find a clear distillation of the ideas that created the American political structure.

The Nineteenth Century

This was the century of "isms" (Positivism, Romanticism, Marxism and so on), a time of searching for some system of thought that would make sense of life's realities. In the wake of Christianity's declining influence in the intellectual sphere, people instead sought for answers in science, political and economic justice, art and nature. The only common element to these searches was their failure to provide a satisfying alternative to the Christian faith. Many of the issues raised in their inquiries, however, must be grappled with by Christians who wish to bring the lordship of Christ to bear on all life.

WOLFGANG VON GOETHE (1749-1832)
Faust
Sorrows of the Young Werther

As important to German culture as Shakespeare was to England, Goethe excelled in almost every literary genre he attempted. These studies of the temptation of knowledge *(Faust)* and despair *(Werther)* are good places to start. Goethe was a humanist who practiced the religion of the self and believed in redemption through expanding one's own personality.

GEORG WILHELM FRIEDRICH HEGEL (1770-1831)
The Phenomenology of Spirit

Hegel's almost unreadable philosophical text contains many interesting ideas. It is, however, difficult to sort them out in the dense thicket of his writing style. This work, nonetheless, has had a profound influence on modern philosophy.

WILLIAM WORDSWORTH (1770-1850)
Poems

This English Romantic poet, who had a deep love for nature and a concern for the spiritual life of mankind, was deeply influenced by a Platonic form of Christian thought. His magnificent poems are rich, powerful and memorable.

> Our birth is but a sleep and a forgetting:
> The Soul that rises with us, our life's Star,
> > Hath had elsewhere its setting,
> > And cometh from afar.
> Not in entire forgetfulness,
> And not in utter nakedness
> But trailing clouds of glory do we come
> > From God, who is our home:
> Heaven lies about us in our infancy!
> Shades of the prison-house begin to close
> > Upon the growing Boy.
> WILLIAM WORDSWORTH, "Ode: Intimations of Immortality"

STENDHAL (1783-1842)
The Red and the Black

A thoroughly engaging novel about a young man who uses all means necessary to advance his own position in life. A well-drawn slice of life in eighteenth- and nineteenth-century France.

LORD BYRON [GEORGE GORDON] (1788-1824)
Poems

Byron was perhaps better known for his rakish lifestyle than for his poems. They are, nonetheless, passionate and worthy of attention.

PERCY BYSSHE SHELLEY (1792-1822)
Poems

Shelley's deeply felt atheism is one of the factors that make his poems original and memorable. He is one of the most intellectually challenging of the English Romantic poets.

JOHN KEATS (1795-1821)
Poems

A fine English poet from the century that produced so many, Keats mixes a classical restraint with an interest in supernatural and spiritualistic themes.

MARY SHELLEY (1797-1851)
Frankenstein

A powerful novel and a cautionary tale about the egotistic ambitions of human beings who seek to play God. Not to be confused with the Frankenstein movies of the 1930s, this is a very serious, beautifully written and profound work.

HONORÉ BALZAC (1799-1850)
Pere Goirot

One of the better novels by this prolific French writer, *Pere Goirot* is filled with wonderful character studies and well-drawn cultural background. Balzac attempted to capture an entire world in his many novels and short stories. Dante wrote the *Divine Comedy;* Balzac attempted to chronicle the "human comedy." *Pere Goirot* is a good place to start exploring his world.

VICTOR HUGO (1802-1885)
Les Miserables

This long but powerful novel set in France is worth the effort it takes to read; it reveals both the pains and joys of existence. Inspector Javert's unflinching pursuit of the humble and repentant thief is a story of heroism, injustice, love and the limits of revenge. This is one of those few novels that are better read in an abridgment, as Hugo has a tendency to wax eloquent and write at length about matters peripheral to the story. But don't let that scare you away from a wonderful reading experience.

RALPH WALDO EMERSON (1803-1882)
Essays and Sermons

An American philosopher and pundit of the transcendental school, Emerson has deeply influenced the popular American consciousness and affected the way, for better or worse, that many people think about religion and ethics.

> Whoso would be a man, must be a nonconformist. He who would gather immortal palms must not be hindered by the name of goodness, but must explore if it be goodness. Nothing is at last sacred but the integrity of your own mind.
>
> A man is to carry himself in the presence of opposition as if every thing were titular and ephemeral but he. I am ashamed to think how easily we capitulate to badges and names, to large societies and dead institutions.
>
> RALPH WALDO EMERSON, *On Self Reliance*

NATHANIEL HAWTHORNE (1804-1864)
The Scarlet Letter

One of the seminal works of American literature, *The Scarlet Letter* presents an unflattering view of the Puritans. The story is immensely powerful and humanely told, stirring sympathy for Hawthorne's unfortunate characters. Such themes as guilt, confession and forgiveness are forcefully portrayed in this novel.

ALEXIS DE TOCQUEVILLE (1805-1873)
Democracy in America

This French writer traveled throughout America and recorded his thoughts and predictions concerning this then-young country. A perceptive observer and sage analyst, he was astoundingly prophetic.

JOHN STUART MILL (1806-1873)
On Liberty
The Subjection of Women
Autobiography

Mill's call for tolerance and liberty is as relevant now as it was when he penned it. His writing style is graceful and his exposition clear and thought provoking. Mill was certainly one of the greatest and most gifted men of the nineteenth century.

> It is a piece of idle sentimentality that truth, merely as truth, has any inherent power denied to error or prevailing against the dungeon and the stake. Men are not more zealous for truth than they often are for error.
>
> The real advantage which truth has consists in this, that when an opinion is true, it may be extinguished once, twice, or many times, but in the course of ages there will generally be found persons to rediscover it.
>
> JOHN STUART MILL, *On Liberty*

CHARLES DARWIN (1809-1882)
The Origin of Species
The Descent of Man

These two works summarize the findings of Darwin and explain his theory of evolution. Darwin's critics should note the caution with which many of his ideas are expressed. This is at variance with many modern evolutionists, who tend to treat the theory as a proven fact. There are many shamelessly poor critiques of Darwinism on the market. One that deserves attention for its accuracy, tone and scientific respectability is Phillip Johnson's *Darwin on Trial.*

EDGAR ALLAN POE (1809-1849)
Short Stories

Poe had a grasp of the diabolical and the horrible that somehow makes his strange tales very convincing. His style is so lyrical that even the most unthinkable events are cast in a strangely fascinating light.

CHARLES DICKENS (1812-1870)
David Copperfield
The Pickwick Papers
Hard Times
A Christmas Carol
A Tale of Two Cities

Dickens could sometimes be faulted for being overlong and sentimental, but his novels lodge in the memory long after they are read. He created a multitude of unforgettable characters. The adjective *Dickensian* can refer to his vivid depictions of poverty-stricken Victorian England; to his intricate, convoluted plots, full of remarkable coincidences; or to jolly and genial scenes of domestic bliss. His staunch Victorian morality is a pleasant contrast to modern-day moral drift.

CHARLOTTE BRONTË (1816-1855)
Jane Eyre

The life of a virtuous and intelligent young woman is captured in this novel, which revolves around one of the most satisfying love stories in literature. This wise book has much to teach us about the nature of real love.

HENRY DAVID THOREAU (1817-1862)
Walden
Civil Disobedience

Thoreau escaped to the world of nature and recorded his observations in *Walden*. What he learned encompasses not only nature itself but also the purpose and conduct of human lives. This beautifully written book is a refreshing tonic for the modern city dweller.

> I went to the woods because I wished to live deliberately, to front only the essential facts of life, and see if I could not learn what it had to teach, and not, when I came to die, discover that I had not lived.
>
> I wanted to live deep and suck out all the marrow of life, to live so sturdily and Spartan-like as to put to rout all that was not life, to cut a broad swath and shave close, to drive life into a corner, and reduce it to its lowest terms, and, if it proved to be mean, why then to get the whole and genuine meanness of it, and publish its meanness to the world; or if it were sublime, to know it by experience and be able to give an account of it. HENRY DAVID THOREAU, *Walden*

EMILY BRONTË (1818-1848)
Wuthering Heights

A haunting story of enduring love and vengeful hatred that has deservedly gained a lasting place in English literature. With deep emotional impact, Brontë explores human nature and its limitations.

IVAN TURGENEV (1818-1883)
Fathers and Sons

This novelistic treatment of the struggle between two generations gave us the word *nihilism,* a term for the philosophy that life is utterly without meaning. Turgenev used the term to capture the ideas of one of the book's main characters.

KARL MARX (1818-1883)
Capital (Das Kapital)
The Communist Manifesto

Capital is an extremely difficult work of economics, but the *Manifesto* is probably the clearest way to get in touch with Marx's major ideas. For Marx on religion, one might want to peruse his "Theses on Feuerbach." For a vitriolic criticism of Marx the man and thinker, see Paul Johnson's chapter on Marx in his book *Intellectuals.*

> The history of all hitherto existing society is the history of class struggles.
>
> The Communists disdain to conceal their views and aims. They openly declare that their ends can be attained only by the forcible overthrow of all existing social conditions. Let the ruling classes tremble at a Communist revolution. The proletarians have nothing to lose but their chains. They have a world to win.
>
> Workingmen of all countries, unite!
>
> KARL MARX (with Frederich Engels), *The Communist Manifesto*

GEORGE ELIOT (1819-1880)
Middlemarch

Writing under a male pseudonym, George Eliot (Mary Ann Evans) was one of the finest female novelists of the nineteenth century. Henry James said of her novels, "There rises from them a kind of fragrance of moral elevation; a love of justice, truth, and light; a large, generous way of looking at things; and a constant effort to hold high the torch in the dusky spaces of man's conscience." *Middlemarch* is built around a well-constructed plot about the pain of lofty goals turned sour by poor choices.

HERMAN MELVILLE (1819-1891)
Moby Dick
Billy Budd

Some sections of *Moby Dick* can prove rather tedious, but when the story finally unravels itself, there is much potent symbolism and some hauntingly good writing in this story about the obsessive pursuit of a whale. *Billy Budd*, a stirring allegorical tale about the trials of a Christlike sailor, is less well known but also well worth reading.

WALT WHITMAN (1819-1892)
Leaves of Grass

This collection of distinctly American poems was written and rewritten throughout Whitman's life. Concerned with self-analysis and self-development, Whitman's poetry predates many modern attitudes about the human soul and spirit.

GUSTAVE FLAUBERT (1821-1880)
Madame Bovary

Written by a French writer of graceful style and penetrating insight, *Madame Bovary* is a gripping novel about the lure and destructiveness of adultery.

CHARLES BAUDELAIRE (1821-1867)
Les fleurs du mal (Flowers of Evil)

The poetry of this French writer is concerned largely with his observations of the dark and degraded side of human nature.

HENRIK IBSEN (1828-1906)
A Doll's House
Hedda Gabler
The Master Builder
The Wild Duck

These gripping tragic dramas deal with the submerged feelings and passions of modern people. Ibsen was ahead of his time in the topicality of his subjects and is considered by many to be one of the finest playwrights of all time.

EMILY DICKINSON (1830-1886)
Poems

Short and highly subjective visions of life by a reclusive woman who saw deeply into nature, other people and herself. Her poetry often seems disarmingly simple, but is highly intellectual and carefully wrought. Many classify

Dickinson as a Christian poet; however, that cannot be determined with certainty. Certainly she did have a strong spiritual element to many of her poems.

> My life closed twice before its close—
> It yet remains to see
> If immortality unveil
> A third event for me
> So huge, so hopeless to conceive
> As these that twice befell.
> Parting is all we know of heaven,
> And all we need of hell. EMILY DICKINSON

LEWIS CARROLL (1832-1898)
Alice's Adventures in Wonderland

A masterpiece of children's literature written by a playful philosophy professor, this book works effectively on many levels. There is definitely more here than initially meets the eye.

MARK TWAIN (1835-1910)
The Adventures of Tom Sawyer
The Adventures of Huckleberry Finn

These roaringly funny and nostalgic novels are so much more than merely "boys' books." Full of beauty and insight into human nature, *Huckleberry Finn* is considered by many to be the greatest American novel. If you enjoy these two, you'll find most of his work worth exploring.

HENRY ADAMS (1838-1919)
The Education of Henry Adams
Mont St. Michel and Chartres

A highly aesthetically driven American author longs for what he considers the good old days: the Middle Ages!

THOMAS HARDY (1840-1928)
Far from the Madding Crowd
Tess of the D'Ubervilles

Tragic and deeply pessimistic, these ultimately powerful novels explore the passions that lie just beneath the surface of tranquil English country life. They reveal a potent vision of a moral universe without God.

WILLIAM JAMES (1842-1910)
Principles of Psychology
Varieties of Religious Experiences

The clearheadedness and pragmatism of James make him an attractive and informative philosopher. His book on religious experience is fascinating and surprisingly sympathetic. It is a must-read for anyone interested in the psychology of religious thought and behavior.

HENRY JAMES (1843-1919)
Portrait of a Lady
Turn of the Screw
Daisy Miller

An American novelist whose power is revealed in the restraint of his writing and his sure sense of observation. *Turn of the Screw* is one of the most famous ghost stories of all time.

OSCAR WILDE (1854-1900)
The Importance of Being Earnest
Lady Windermere's Fan

The exceptionally witty plays by the notorious Oscar Wilde are among the finest comic gems in all of theater. Wilde was a master at wordplay. His haunting novel *The Portrait of Dorian Gray* is also worth investigation.

FRIEDRICH NIETZSCHE (1844-1900)
Beyond Good and Evil
Thus Spake Zarathustra
The Genealogy of Morals

Nietzsche's analysis of what is wrong with the modern world is extremely perceptive, even if his solutions are unacceptable to most believers. Although Nietzsche is, from a biblical viewpoint, wrong in most of the conclusions he draws, he can be exceedingly prophetic in his insights. His books address issues of great importance and can provide excellent tools for helping us examine weaknesses in how we live out our Christian faith.

> "Whither is God?" he cried. "I shall tell you. We have killed him—you and I. All of us are his murderers. But how have we done this? How were we able to drink up the sea? Who gave us the sponge to wipe away the entire horizon? . . . Do we not feel the breath of empty space? Has it not become colder? Is not night and more night coming on all the time? Must not lanterns be lit in the morning? Do we not hear anything yet of the noise of the gravediggers who are burying God? Do we not smell anything yet of God's decomposition? Gods, too, decompose. God is dead. And we have killed him."
>
> FRIEDRICH NIETZSCHE, *Thus Spake Zarathustra*

ROBERT LOUIS STEVENSON (1850-1894)
Dr. Jekyll and Mr. Hyde

This exciting and entertaining tale is also a wonderful parable of the two sides of human nature and how they struggle within an individual's life.

SIGMUND FREUD (1856-1939)
The Interpretation of Dreams
Introductory Lectures of Psychoanalysis
Civilization and Its Discontents

Even his most strident opponents must admit to the brilliance and creativity of Freud's work. Even if we disagree with some of his foundational ideas, we must be captured by his brave attempt to fathom the human psyche. As with other very original writers, much of his work is grossly misunderstood by the general public. See Bruno Bettelheim's sympathetic book *Freud and Man's Soul* for a look at some of these common misconceptions. An excellent critique of Freud from a Christian perspective is the valuable book by Paul C. Vitz, *Sigmund Freud's Christian Unconscious*.

MAX WEBER (1864-1920)
The Protestant Ethic and the Spirit of Capitalism

This groundbreaking sociological study of the Protestant ethic is surprisingly readable and very provocative. Even if you don't agree with Weber's thesis on the Protestant foundation of capitalism (and many scholars do not), you must come to terms with it if you are interested in the questions of economics, work ethics or the nature of capitalism.

STEPHEN CRANE (1871-1900)
The Red Badge of Courage

This short novel captures the horror of the American Civil War as seen through the eyes of a young soldier who is alternately caught up in the excitement of battle and terrified by its ferocity.

The Twentieth Century and Beyond

There is a pervasive note of despair that runs through much of the art, music, literature and philosophy of modern times. In our relativistic age, many people have given up hope of finding any real answers to life's perplexing questions. This has tended to produce work that is intricate, witty or complex on the exterior, but morally hollow at its core. In many ways, we appear to be a culture that is dying, losing that which gave us the strength to achieve much of our greatness. But the despairing voices do us a service in clearly pointing people to their need for the hope and meaning that is available in the gospel.

GEORGE BERNARD SHAW (1856-1950)
Man and Superman
Saint Joan
Arms and the Man
Major Barbara
Heartbreak House

Shaw had a unique gift for dramatizing even the most critical moral and ethical issues in such a way that his plays are extremely insightful, as well as howlingly funny. His more serious philosophical thinking is often undistinguished and unconvincing yet so delightfully articulated that it cannot but capture one's attention.

JOSEPH CONRAD (1857-1924)
The Heart of Darkness

Conrad's haunting vision of the darkness and savagery that lie just below the surface of human civilization makes this a very disturbing book.

ANTON CHEKHOV (1860-1904)
The Cherry Orchard
The Seagull

Two of many great plays by the Russian dramatist whose main focus was on character development rather than a concern for plot.

WILLIAM BUTLER YEATS (1865-1939)
Poems

This great Irish poet was deeply influenced by myth, folklore and a variety of religious traditions. His poetry is full of unforgettable imagery. See especially his haunting vision of the modern world in "The Second Coming."

MARCEL PROUST (1871-1922)
Remembrance of Things Past

A very lengthy and nostalgic novel (in several volumes) demonstrating how the past lives on in the present. Although it is inarguably a major work, many readers will likely find it tedious going at times. A work much praised but little read by anybody except students of French literature.

ROBERT FROST (1874-1963)
Poems

A major American poet whose work is accessible and heartfelt. He is one of those rarest of modern phenomena: a great poet who has been appreciated by a wide audience.

> Two roads diverged in a yellow wood,
> And sorry I could not travel both
> And be one traveler, long I stood
> And looked down one as far as I could
> To where it bent in the undergrowth; . . .
> I shall be telling this with a sigh
> Somewhere ages and ages hence:

Two roads diverged in a wood, and I—
I took the one less traveled by,
And that has made all the difference. ROBERT FROST, "The Road Not Taken"

CARL JUNG (1875-1961)
Modern Man in Search of a Soul

In this book, the great psychologist meditates on the human need for spiritual sustenance in every person's life. Jung's diagnosis is brilliant, though many find his answers to be less than satisfactory. Jung's many contributions to modern psychological thought can be glimpsed in the short guide by Calvin S. Hall and Vernon J. Nordby, *A Primer of Jungian Psychology*. It should be noted that much of Jung's later work veered toward rather occultic themes.

RAINER MARIA RILKE (1875-1926)
Poems
Letters to a Young Poet

Rilke was a German poet who emphasized the importance of beauty in the human life. His poems are lyrical and filled with haunting images. *Letters to a Young Poet* is one of the greatest pieces ever written on the nature and necessity of creativity.

I want to beg you to be patient toward all that is unsolved in your heart and try to love the questions themselves like locked rooms and like books that are written in a very foreign tongue. Do not seek the answers, which cannot be given you because you would not be able to live them. And the point is, to live everything. Live the questions now. Perhaps you will then, gradually, without noticing it, live along some distant day into the answer. RAINER MARIA RILKE, *Letters to a Young Poet*

THOMAS MANN (1875-1955)
The Magic Mountain
Death in Venice

Mann writes persuasively about the decay that is rotting away our civilization. A writer of immense intelligence and deep philosophical concerns, many consider him to be among the best modern writers.

JACK LONDON (1876-1916)
Call of the Wild

Set in the Great North, this adventure tale of a sled dog and the trials of his difficult existence is a delight for readers of all ages.

HERMANN HESSE (1877-1962)
Siddhartha
Steppenwolf
Narcissus and Goldmund

Hesse, most of whose works revolve around the spiritual journey of their central character, is capable of both profound symbolism and beautiful lyrical writing. These three books show this combination at its best. *Siddhartha* is the story of the Buddha, and *Steppenwolf* is a fascinating and eccentric novelistic critique of contemporary culture and its values. *Narcissus and Goldmund* deals unforgettably with the ever-present human struggle between reason and passion.

MARTIN BUBER (1878-1965)
I and Thou

This Jewish theologian and philosopher stresses the need to address God and others as a *Thou*, emphasizing personal encounter with God and those around us.

E. M. FORSTER (1879-1970)
A Passage to India

The clash of cultures in British India is the subject of this book. It provides interesting insights into Hinduism and the many difficulties posed by the cultural clashes brought about as a result of British imperialism.

ALBERT EINSTEIN (1879-1955)
The Meaning of Relativity

Who better to provide a clear explanation of the theory of relativity than the man who formulated it?

JAMES JOYCE (1882-1941)
Portrait of the Artist as a Young Man
Ulysses

A highly original modern writer, Joyce charted a whole new way of portraying reality in literature through his use of stream of consciousness. *Ulysses* is a very long novel that explores a single day in the life of an Irish man. Immensely influential, though few have successfully attempted to carry the experiment to the lengths he did. A decidedly cerebral writer, Joyce wrote with a great deal of passion and, at times, a soaring lyricism.

> History, Stephen said, is a nightmare from which I am trying to awake.
> JAMES JOYCE, *Ulysses*

VIRGINIA WOOLF (1882-1941)
Mrs. Dalloway
To the Lighthouse

Woolf wrote difficult and highly subjective novels that experiment with the stream-of-consciousness mode of writing.

FRANZ KAFKA (1883-1924)
The Trial
The Castle
The Metamorphosis

The nightmarish world of Kafka is unforgettable. He writes of a world without God, where humans are victims of themselves and their deep confusions. If there is no God, ultimately Kafka's vision is right. If there is a God, then he shows us clearly what the gospel rescues us from.

D. H. LAWRENCE (1885-1930)
Sons and Lovers
Women in Love

A fine writer whose fixation on the necessity of nurturing the sexual instinct made him a hero to some and anathema to others. Even those who find his philosophy of life somewhat lacking in depth (including me) must admit that he has highlighted many human concerns often ignored by polite society. Lawrence poses many good questions but mostly arrives at answers that are too earth-bound.

EUGENE O'NEILL (1888-1953)
Long Day's Journey into Night
The Iceman Cometh

These are powerful dramas about human degradation and despair; they show the dehumanizing effects of certain trends in modern culture.

ALDOUS HUXLEY (1894-1963)
Brave New World

An anti-utopian novel about the suffocating nightmare of a pleasure-driven existence in a not-too-distant future. In fact, with every year that passes, the book seems to become more frighteningly relevant.

JAMES THURBER (1894-1961)
The Thurber Carnival

One of the finest American humorists reflects on life and its absurdities with hilarious results. It would be hard to pick a favorite story from this consistently entertaining collection.

F. SCOTT FITZGERALD (1896-1940)
The Great Gatsby

An influential novel of love and death in the flapper era, rich in symbolism and carefully written.

ERICH MARIA REMARQUE (1898-1970)
All Quiet on the Western Front

This gripping short novel vividly captures the horrors experienced by soldiers on the front lines and in the trenches of the First World War. Those interested in further pursuit of this issue might want to read Paul Fussell's fascinating study, *The Great War and Modern Memory*.

THORNTON WILDER (1897-1975)
Our Town

Wilder's drama seems simple on the surface but has much to say about the human condition. Readers might also want to try his novel *The Bridge of San Luis Rey*, which is a convincing portrayal of God's superintendence over human existence.

WILLIAM FAULKNER (1897-1962)
The Sound and the Fury
As I Lay Dying

Be forewarned: Faulkner is not easy to read. His richly experimental prose will yield gems to the patient reader, but will be merely an annoyance to those who read primarily for plot. Take the necessary effort, and you will glean much from this master of human psychology. His carefully constructed characters and the rural Southern setting both come unforgettably alive.

BERTOLT BRECHT (1898-1956)
The Caucasian Chalk Circle
Mother Courage and Her Children

Brecht was an influential political dramatist of the left, whose dramas bring to life major social and political concerns.

ERNEST HEMINGWAY (1899-1961)
For Whom the Bell Tolls
The Sun Also Rises
The Old Man and the Sea

Hemingway's writing is characterized by a spare and unadorned style, a good deal of bravado and an underlying sense of existential despair. He's a good storyteller, but his literary reputation has fluctuated over time. Perhaps his greatest asset as a writer is the sharpness of his prose, which he took great pains to make clear, realistic and free of excessive ornamentation.

ZORA NEAL HURSTON (CA. 1900-1960)
Their Eyes Were Watching God

A delightful and entertaining novel by one of the best African American writers. Written with the flavor of a folk tale but with an eye to very contemporary concerns.

JOHN STEINBECK (1902-1968)
The Grapes of Wrath
The Pearl

The Grapes of Wrath is the moving story of a family of "Okies" who leave the dust bowl and travel to California in search of a better life but do not find the promised land they expected. Steinbeck's *The Pearl* is a shorter work, reflective of one of Christ's parables.

GEORGE ORWELL (1903-1950)
1984
Animal Farm

Orwell's powerful writing demonstrates his impatience with the tyrannical tendencies of both the political right (fascism) and left (communism). Both of these works are frightening and prophetic, yet show evidence of an underlying belief in the dignity of every human being.

JEAN PAUL SARTRE (1905-1980)
Nausea
No Exit
Being and Nothingness

Most readers will find Sartre's philosophical writings, such as *Being and Nothingness*, rather impenetrable, but the essence of his despairing and suffocating vision is captured well in his novels and plays. Here is an acute vision of a world without God and without ultimate hope.

VIKTOR FRANKL (1905-1997)
Man's Search for Meaning

An important work of nonfiction by a psychiatrist who, using his own experiences in a Nazi concentration camp, diagnoses humankind's most basic need as finding meaning in life. Frankl launched a psychological school of thought called "logotherapy," a method with important ramifications for Christian psychologists.

SAMUEL BECKETT (1906-1989)
Waiting for Godot
Endgame

Beckett's despairing view of human existence is well captured in these two plays. In a universe without God, Beckett's characters lead pointless, doomed lives. Very short on plot, these plays are saved from ponderousness by Beckett's droll sense of humor.

ALBERT CAMUS (1913-1960)
The Stranger
The Plague
The Myth of Sisyphus

Two very powerful novels and a philosophical essay by a French existentialist who called for human dignity and hope, even in an incomprehendable world. Camus is a fine writer and gives the reader much food for thought. The best place to start exploring his work is probably with *The Plague*.

> There is but one truly serious philosophical problem, and that is suicide. Judging whether life is or is not worth living amounts to answering the fundamental question of philosophy. ALBERT CAMUS, *The Myth of Sisyphus*

> Can one be a saint without God: this is the only concrete problem I know today. ALBERT CAMUS, *The Plague*

THOMAS S. KUHN (1922-1996)
The Structure of Scientific Revolutions

Kuhn is a powerful tonic for those who believe that science is a completely objective tool for discovering truth. Demolishing the fallacy of logical positivism, he shows how science is dependent on nonrational procedures and is limited by the prevailing scientific paradigms of its day. A powerful corrective for those who put undue trust in the results of science.

TENNESSEE WILLIAMS (1914-1983)
The Glass Menagerie
A Streetcar Named Desire

Williams's dramas are filled with well-conceived characters in an atmosphere of sadness, hopelessness and despair.

ARTHUR MILLER (1915-)
Death of a Salesman

A powerful play by one of the most accomplished dramatists of our time. The drama centers on a man trapped in an unhappy and meaningless existence.

EDWARD ALBEE (1928-)
Who's Afraid of Virginia Woolf?

A brutal and searing drama about misunderstanding, psychological breakdown and the "games people play," this play is fascinating and repelling at the same time.

Great Books of the East

The books listed in this chapter have come exclusively from the Western world. But as the cultural distances in our world continue to shrink due to improvements in technology and communication, we must become increasingly aware of traditions other than our own. If you are a Westerner interested in books from a tradition very different from your own, try this handful of great books from the East.

Confucius (551-479 B.C.), *The Analects* (aphorisms and teachings of the Chinese founder of Confucianism)

Sun-tzu (ca. 450-380 B.C.), *The Art of War* (written by a Chinese philosopher and military strategist)

Mencius (ca. 400-320 B.C.), *The Book of Mencius* (the other great philosopher of Confucianism)

Valmiki (ca. 300 B.C.), *The Ramayana* (an Ancient Indian epic religious poem)

Vyasa (ca. 200 B.C.), *The Mahabharata* (a long epic poem of dynastic warfare from India)

Unknown (ca. 200 B.C.), *The Bhagavad Gita* (an important religious poem from India)

Kalidasa (ca. 400 A.D.), *Sakuntala* (a drama from the playwright known as "the Shakespeare of India")

Muhammad (ca. 650), the Qur'an (the holy book of Islam)

Hui-Neng (638-713) *The Platform Sutra of the Sixth Patriarch* (an important work of Buddhist teaching)

Lady Murasaki (ca. 976-1015), *The Tale of Genji* (many critics consider this Japanese work one of the greatest novels of all time)

Omar Khayyam (ca. 1050), *The Rubaiyat* (a Persian poem with Islamic philosophy)

Matsuo Basho (1644-1694), *The Narrow Road to the Deep North* (the travel record of the most famous Chinese haiku poet)

Ts'ao Hsueh-ch'in (1715-1763), *The Dream of the Red Chamber* (generally considered the finest work of fiction in Chinese literature)

Soseki Natsume (1867-1916), *Kokoro* (considered by many to be the first major modern Japanese novel)

Yasunari Kawabata (1899-1972), *Beauty and Sadness* (a beautifully written modern Japanese novel)

FIVE

EXPLORING POETRY

What images does the word *poetry* conjure up in your mind? A besotted suitor speaking forth the glories of his beloved in treacly verse?

A bespectacled teacher droning on about the twenty-seventh stanza of an epic poem concerning the ruins of some ancient city?

Or is it rather the joy of sitting under a tree in the fall, turning the pages of a book of poems and feeling as though your heart has been lifted up to a realm of beauty where everything around you seems to bask in the glow of some luminous transcendent light?

There is plenty of bad poetry around—poetry that is maudlin and sentimental and inauthentic. But I've discovered that there is also poetry that can enrich my life; that can be source of beauty and insight and pleasure. One of the great joys of reading, I've learned, is coming to see the richness and splendor of great poetry. If you struggled through lessons in poetry appreciation in high school and drew the conclusion that poetry was not for you, perhaps it's time to investigate again. You might just find yourself joining those who have discovered the wonder that comes from listening to the poet.

Following are listed some books about poetry to help orient you, as well as two anthologies. After that are two lists of poets whose work is worth exploring, some of whom I have discussed in previous chapters.

Books About Poetry

EDWARD HIRSCH
How to Read a Poem, and Fall in Love with Poetry

It is evident from the very first pages of this book that you are reading the words of someone who cherishes poetry and wants to introduce you to the object of his intense affection. Hirsch is especially helpful in pointing to the role of the poetry reader as a "co-creator" with the poet and in endorsing Emily Dickinson's contention that poetry has a place in developing the soul. In fact, Hirsch compares the act of reading poetry to prayer. This is a rich introduction to reading and enjoying poetry.

J. D. MCCLATCHY
Twenty Questions

This is not only a book about poetry, it is a book by someone who is obviously a poet himself. With masterly and sometimes sensuous images, McClatchy responds to twenty questions about poets and poetry, contemplating the role that poetry plays in life and pointing us to some of his favorite poets.

MOLLY PEACOCK
How to Read a Poem . . . and Start a Poetry Circle

Collecting the poems that come to mean something special to you, claims Ms. Peacock, gives the reader "a special hold on life." She urges readers to begin to discover their own set of favorite poems and to share them with others. Along the way, she shares personal reflections of some of her favorite poems and their creators.

MICHAEL SCHMIDT
Lives of the Poets

At nearly one thousand pages, *Lives of the Poets* may look like a textbook, but it certainly doesn't read like one. Written with a light touch and obvious love of poetry, this book connects the lives and work of over three hundred English-speaking poets in a lively mixture of biography, history and literary criticism. *Lives of the Poets* is organized in such a way that you can read it cover to cover or browse to read about your favorite poets. A wonderful, accessible and comprehensive guided tour of the world of poetry.

Two Favorite Poetry Anthologies

WILLIAM HARMON, EDITOR
The Top 500 Poems

Harmon studied over four hundred anthologies of poetry to see which poems were the most commonly anthologized. The result was this compilation of the five hundred greatest poems in the English language. Then he arranged them chronologically and added a short introduction to each poem. The result is the best single anthology of poetry I've ever come across. These five hundred poems are a great starting place for reacquainting yourself with old favorites and discovering some poems and poets you didn't know. If you own only one book of poetry, this is the one to own.

JAMES H. TROTT, EDITOR
A Sacrifice of Praise

Helpful introductions enhance this massive collection of the best Christian poetry through the ages, from Caedmon to moderns like Luci Shaw and Denise Levertov. Organized in chronological order, it is a demonstration of the richness of our Christian heritage in verse. On the following page is a list of key poems to explore, drawn from this work.

THE POETS
The Classic Poets

Francesco Petrarch

John Donne

Henry Vaughn

William Blake

Robert Burns

Samuel Taylor Coleridge

Percy Bysshe Shelley

Ralph Waldo Emerson

Henry Wadsworth Longfellow

Alfred Lord Tennyson

Robert Browning

Emily Dickinson

William Shakespeare

George Herbert

Thomas Traherne

John Milton

William Wordsworth

George Gordon (Lord Byron)

John Keats

Elizabeth Barrett Browning

Edgar Allan Poe

Charles Baudelaire

Walt Whitman

Christina Rossetti

Modern Poets

Thomas Hardy

William Butler Yeats

Robert Frost

William Carlos Williams

T. S. Eliot

Wilfred Owen

Dylan Thomas

Pablo Neruda

Gerard Manley Hopkins

Rainer Maria Rilke

Langston Hughes

Ezra Pound

e. e. cummings

W. H. Auden

Allen Ginsburg

A Handful of My Favorite Contemporary Poets

Czeslaw Milosz

Denise Levertov

Wendell Berry

Kelly Cherry

Steve Turner

R. S. Thomas

Seamus Heany

Luci Shaw

Scott Cairns

S I X

BOOKS TO HELP YOU
THINK LIKE A CHRISTIAN

Many Christians have a tendency to think about their faith primarily in terms of their personal experience with God. For them, faith is mostly about feeling and commitment, or possibly about holding onto a family tradition of belief. Of course, each of these things is a valid part of the Christian experience, but we should never forget that Christianity is not only a way of feeling, but it is also a way of seeing and understanding the world. Ultimately, Christianity is a complete and unified philosophy of life.

Some readers might shrink from the word *philosophy*, fearful of an emphasis upon abstract ideas that don't have much to do with the actual living out of life. So let us use another word, one that thinkers like Francis Schaeffer have used so effectively: *worldview*.

A worldview is a set of beliefs about reality that have an impact on every area of our life. It deals with such questions as Is there a God? If so, how can we know him? What is the nature of humankind? What is truth? What is our purpose in life? The way we answer these questions will affect the way we view almost every area of our lives: ethics, politics, science, the arts, culture and relationships. If we have committed ourselves to be followers of Jesus Christ, our responses to these questions are important.

They will influence our faithfulness and also our ability to communicate the gospel to our neighbor. Because we live in a culture that is sometimes not very receptive to the Christian faith, we must make the effort to think through the meaning of our faith. We must ask ourselves about its content (what does a Christian believe?), and we must ask what kind of difference it makes on how we think about our lives and the decisions we face every day.

In the lists that follow, I've tried to suggest some books that will be helpful for gaining a clearer understanding of the content of faith (theology), some books that defend the reasonableness of faith (apologetics) and some books that explore the impact of a Christian commitment on such areas as culture, history, science and the arts. Of course, one could also create lists on such specific subjects as sociology, psychology, education, politics and so on. I've chosen to focus on the areas I know best, but many books in the various lists below include valuable bibliographies for those who want to explore another area in greater depth. In making my recommendations, I have tried mostly to select books that communicate clearly to the layperson, books that don't require a lot of background in the subject area. I hope these lists will be helpful in building a more solid intellectual base for your faith.

Developing a Christian Worldview

HARRY BLAMIRES
The Christian Mind

A former student of C. S. Lewis, Blamires provides here a clear presentation of the primary presuppositions of the Christian worldview. A good basic book for understanding how being a Christian should affect the way you view all kinds of different issues.

CHARLES COLSON
How Now Shall We Live?

This is, in many ways, Colson's magnum opus, a grand summary of what it means to think like a Christian. Committed to the idea that the meaning of Christianity goes far beyond the salvation experience, Colson demonstrates the importance of developing a Christian worldview. In some five hundred pages, Colson provides the understanding you'll need to think through how faith affects every arena of thought and life. Although based on extensive research, Colson's book is anything but pedantic. Written in a clear and interesting manner, and illustrated with gripping stories of real women and men of the past and present, *How Now Shall We Live?* is an engaging introduction to what it means to have a truly Christian mind. Highly recommended. (Some other Colson books are listed below and in chapter seven.)

> The term *worldview* may sound abstract or philosophical, a topic discussed by pipe-smoking, tweed-jacketed professors in academic settings. But actually a person's worldview is intensely practical. It is simply the sum total of our beliefs about the world, the "big picture" that directs our daily decisions and actions. And understanding worldviews is extremely important. . . . Genuine Christianity is a way of seeing and comprehending all reality. It is a worldview.
> CHARLES COLSON, *How Now Shall We Live?*

C. S. LEWIS
Mere Christianity

If you could only read one book other than the Bible to gain an understanding of what the Christian faith is all about, I cannot think of a better choice than *Mere Christianity.* As one reviewer suggested, it is a great book for anyone who wants to be a Christian but finds his or her mind getting in the way. Lewis's winsome, logical, commonsense approach to faith has had a considerable impact upon countless believers, helping them to understand what the Christian faith teaches and how to live that faith out on a day-to-day basis. If you haven't read it yet, you've missed out on one of the greatest Christian books ever written. (Other books by Lewis are recommended in this chapter and chapters three and seven.)

JAMES SIRE
The Universe Next Door
How to Read Slowly
Habits of the Mind

James Sire has probably done more to popularize the idea of the worldview than any other contemporary writer. When I was a young believer with lots of questions, his books helped me immensely in my search to understand how Christianity fit into the marketplace of ideas. In a clear and concise manner *The Universe Next Door* explores the content of the Christian worldview and compares its presuppositions with other competing world-views, such as deism, naturalism, nihilism, existentialism, pantheism and new consciousness. Well-organized chapters help readers to identify the worldviews that lurk behind all kinds of contemporary ideas. In *How to Read Slowly*, Sire teaches us how to be better and more discerning readers by learning to identify the worldviews behind the books we read. *Habits of the Mind* is a more recent book, and it talks about the whole cluster of issues that surround what it means to have a Christian mind. Filled with lots of good advice for becoming a better thinker and reader, Sire proves once again that he is an exceptionally fine teacher.

DANIEL TAYLOR
The Myth of Certainty

This is one of my favorite books to give to people who want to think a little more deeply about their Christian commitment. In it Daniel Taylor calls for humility in the way we understand our faith. It is too easy for us to become convinced that we've got it all figured out and that Christianity has an easy answer to every question we face. But when we believe this "myth of certainty," we are only fooling ourselves. While we may be able to give a logical explanation for much of what we believe—and trying to do that is always worthwhile—Taylor reminds us that even the wisest and most intelligent will have to learn to live with uncertainty and mystery. But the glorious truth he reminds us of is this: we can be committed disciples even when we don't have everything figured out.

> Consider the television preacher and how fearfully he is made. I do not abuse him for being on television—it is the highest hill around. I do not complain that he asks for money—he has many barns to build. I allow him even his politics and prejudices (even as I wince when he makes them God's) because I have my politics and prejudices as well. But I do stand amazed at one thing. Where, someone tell me, did he get this brimming confidence? Not his confidence before men and women—the psychology of that I can understand—but this confidence before God. Did *he* talk to a burning bush? Is he certain his sacrifice is not a stench in

God's nostrils? Why are there no signs of ashes on his head? Why does he seem unconcerned with such questions? Even "send me" Isaiah despaired of his unclean lips. DANIEL TAYLOR, *The Myth of Certainty*

Theology and Apologetics

DIOGENES ALLEN
Christian Belief in a Postmodern World

In this book Diogenes Allen, a philosophy professor at Princeton, grapples with the issue of how Christian thinkers should respond to the new intellectual environment created by the rise of postmodernism and religious pluralism. And while many Christian apologists have focused on constructing a critique of this new mindset, Allen takes a different approach—he looks for the positive insights that can be gleaned from the postmodern approach. Allen shows that rather than fearing contemporary thinking, we can look to the latest findings of science and philosophy for confirmation of the reality of God, and to other faiths to understand our own more deeply. A provocative and invigorating study.

PETER BERGER
A Rumor of Angels

Peter Berger, one of today's most respected sociologists, offers a defense for the reality of the supernatural through an understanding of the sociology of knowledge. Through a dialogue with sociologists, philosophical anthropologists and theologians, Berger lays out the case for a way out of the impasse of materialism. And though one might expect this kind of argument to be weighted down with impenetrable academic language and philosophical abstraction, Berger clearly, gracefully and wittily guides readers through the twists and turns of his logic. *A Rumor of Angels* is a brilliant and essential study for anyone interested in transcending the usual approaches of apologetics. Explore *The Sacred Canopy* and *The Heretical Imperative* for further Berger insights into the field of religion and sociology.

DONALD BLOESCH
Essentials of Evangelical Theology (two volumes)

There are two aspects to Bloesch's work that make him my favorite contemporary theologian. First, his knowledge and the breadth of his reading are staggering. Unlike many theologians, who seem to confine their study to their own tradition, Bloesch has a keen awareness of what others are thinking. He has read and interacted with thinkers of many traditions, trying to sort out the implications of their thought on contemporary evangelical theology. He's also not afraid to use the insights of those outside of the professional theological world. For example, he wisely uses insights from one of C. S. Lewis's fictional works to discuss the nature of sin. Second, Bloesch is a wonderful synthesizer. He always seems to find a way to balance the competing sides of every issue, joining seemingly conflicting ideas together in fresh but still orthodox ways. The two volumes of *Essentials of Evangelical Theology* are a great place to start, but Bloesch is also working on a multivolume series (Christian Foundations) that will explore the key aspects of the Christian faith in greater depth.

RON FROST
Discover the Power of the Bible

This wise little volume is a perfect introduction for the person new to the Bible. In it Frost offers a basic understanding of how to approach Scripture and gives a concise overview to the message of the Bible and how all its parts fit together. The capstone of the book is his suggestion that we need to begin to read the Bible as we would any other book. Instead of poring over it verse by verse, we should simply read large portions at a sitting and allow ourselves to be transformed in the process.

CARL F. H. HENRY
God, Revelation and Authority

Carl Henry is one of the great minds of modern evangelicalism, one of the founders of *Christianity Today* magazine and one of the most vocal proponents of a more intellectually respectable proclamation of the gospel. His legacy to the evangelical community is immense. *God, Revelation and Authority* is his massive statement of evangelical theology. Stretching to six fat volumes, Henry's work answers the objections of the critics against the authority and inerrancy of Scripture and restates traditional theology in an intellectually satisfying manner. It will undoubtedly continue to stand as a landmark for future evangelical theologians.

D. JAMES KENNEDY AND JERRY NEWCOMBE
What If Jesus Had Never Been Born?

This book has an interesting thesis: how would our world be different if Jesus had never entered it? In the process of answering that question, Kennedy and Newcombe have given a positive angle to apologetics, pointing out all the important ways that the Christian faith has influenced such areas as education, morality, science, medicine, the arts, political philosophy and many other areas. Their message is pragmatic—Christianity works; it has created a better world for us to live in. Although I take issue with the tendency of the authors to overstate their case at times, the book is provocative and suggests a valuable direction for those who are interested in defending the gospel.

PETER KREEFT
Between Heaven and Hell
Handbook of Christian Apologetics (with Ronald Tacelli)
Making Sense Out of Suffering
Christianity for Modern Pagans

Kreeft is one of the most popular defenders of the faith writing today. He marshals his wit and creativity to great effect in his effort to show the intellectual respectability of the Christian faith. A natural teacher, he is easy to follow and provides the kind of word pictures that help you remember what he has imparted. *Between Heaven and Hell* is a fictional imagining of a conversation that might have taken place between three famous men who all died on the same day: C. S. Lewis, John F. Kennedy and British pantheistic philosopher Aldous Huxley. Somewhere between heaven and hell, as they await their final destination, these three brilliant minds debate the ultimate questions of life. It is a perfect method for showing the differences between three very major competing worldviews. *Handbook of Christian Apologetics* is a more prosaic work, a clear and well-organized guide to the basic issues of Christian apologetics. *Christianity for Modern Pagans* is Kreeft's guidebook to the greatest apologist of all time—Blaise Pascal. His reflections on Pascal's thought are sure to make this important thinker come alive to the modern reader. Finally, *Making Sense Out of Suffering* is probably the best work I've read on the problem of reconciling God's love with the pain in our world. Looking for clues to this mystery, he never makes the mistake of sounding as if he has everything figured out, but he is always helpful and compassionate.

> No computer, or artificial intelligence, either weeps or wonders. . . . They do not question their programming, unless you program them to do that, and then they do not question *that* programming. We too have been programmed by our heredity and environment, but we question our programming. We doubt. Doubt is glorious. Only one who can doubt can believe, just as only one who can despair can hope, and only one who can hate can love. . . . No angel, spirit, god, or goddess suffers or questions, weeps or wonders. . . . We alone, we humans, weep and wonder. PETER KREEFT, *Making Sense Out of Suffering*

HANS KÜNG
On Being a Christian
Does God Exist?

Although one can argue that Küng gives too much ground to modernism in his attempt to make Christianity relevant to the modern world, he is an example of that rarest of creatures: a top-notch scholar who is able to write books that are clear, entertaining and relevant. His long-term battle against the doctrine of papal infallibility has earned him a censure from the Vatican, but he remains among the most influential of modern Catholic theologians. Even the reader whose theology is more conservative will find his books packed with acute insights and a deep historical understanding. In my estimation, *Does God Exist?* is one of the most impressive works of modern religious philosophy and a stunning work of apologetics.

C. S. LEWIS
Mere Christianity
The Problem of Pain
God in the Dock

We've already discussed *Mere Christianity* under another heading (Christian Worldview), but it is also worth pointing out two other excellent Lewis books on apologetics-related issues. *The Problem of Pain* is a classic on why pain and suffering exist in a world created by a loving God. *God in the Dock* is a collection of essays on many theological and apologetical issues.

PAUL LITTLE
Know What You Believe
Know Why You Believe

These two long-time bestsellers do a great job of summarizing the basics of theology and defending the intellectual respectability of faith. They are a solid resource for the beginning reader in theology and apologetics.

GERALD R. MCDERMOTT
Can Evangelicals Learn from World Religions?

One question that vexes a lot of thinking Christians has to do with the relationship between Christianity and the other major world religions. What should our attitude be toward other faiths? Is there anything we can learn from them? In this well-argued book, McDermott finds a place of balance in answers to these questions while remaining committed to the Christian faith.

JOSH MCDOWELL
Evidence That Demands a Verdict
More Than a Carpenter

Designed as a tool for those who are sharing their faith with skeptics, *Evidence That Demands a Verdict* remains as valuable as it was when it was originally published. Although not written in the typical paragraph-by-paragraph form of most books, its outlined format is probably one of the things that make it most useful. And for countless believers it has inspired confidence in the intellectual respectability of faith and the dependability of the Bible. *More Than a Carpenter* is a handy distillation of *Evidence That Demands a Verdict*.

ALISTER MCGRATH
Intellectuals Don't Need God and Other Modern Myths
The Unknown God

McGrath is one of the most prolific modern evangelical writers, and what is amazing is the consistent quality of his books. Although he has penned some well-respected academic tomes, his passion seems to be for making theology interesting and accessible to the common person. He's written on all kinds of topics, but the two volumes recommended here are good places to start. *Intellectuals Don't Need God* is a readable refutation of the attacks that have been leveled against Christianity by its opponents, well organized and with an attempt to get at the real questions, not just the ones that Christians find easy to answer. *The Unknown God* is designed to be a book for a skeptic or nonbeliever and attempts to lay out the meaning of faith in a clear way, illustrated with photographs and classic art. After you've perused these two books, you'll want to explore other books by this important writer.

J. P. MORELAND
Scaling the Secular City
Writing here for serious students of apologetics, Moreland has created a comprehensive guide to the basic issues and how addressing them can help make our presentation of the gospel more effective to the modern mind.

J. I. PACKER
Knowing God
Countless Christians have turned to this modern classic as a guide to a basic understanding of their faith and help in growing stronger. A work of applied theology, it helps readers understand how to better live out a faith that is more than just a cluster of intellectual ideas. Packer points again and again to the importance of not just knowing *about* God, but knowing him in an intimate relationship. The book's survey of the basics has earned it a place in the hearts of many for its clarity and sound orthodoxy.

R. C. SPROUL
If There's a God, Then Why Are There Atheists?
Many critics of Christianity have used psychology to explain the allure of faith. They have suggested that those who embrace faith do so out of a sense of psychological need, hoping to demonstrate by this that faith is more of a psychological crutch than an intellectual commitment. In this book, noted popular theologian Sproul turns the tables on that argument,

uncovering the common psychological patterns for nonbelief, constructing thereby a psychologically based critique of atheism. This brilliant little volume will prove very helpful in your discussions with those who have decided that God does not exist.

HELMUT THIELICKE
The Evangelical Faith (three volumes)
How the World Began
A Little Exercise for Young Theologians

For a full appreciation of Thielicke, see the annotation under his work in chapter three. The three books listed here repay careful reading. *The Evangelical Faith* is his systematic theology, filled with profound insights, but not an easy read. More readable are his collection of sermons on the book of Genesis *(How the World Began)* and his remarkable little guidebook for beginning students of theology, *A Little Exercise for Young Theologians*. No one has ever done a better job of pointing out the necessity for humility in undertaking the theological enterprise than Thielicke does in that small volume.

> There is a hiatus between the arena of the young theologian's actual spiritual growth and what he already knows intellectually about this arena. . . . In his book on Goethe, Gundolf speaks, in reference to such cases, of a merely conceptual experience. Some truth or the other has not been "passed through" as a primary experience, but has been replaced by a "perception" of the literary or intellectual deposit of what another's primary experience, say Luther's, has discovered. Thus one lives at second hand.
>
> HELMUT THIELICKE, *A Little Exercise for Young Theologians*

JIM THOMAS
Coffeehouse Theology

Have you ever wished you had a trusted friend with whom you could sit down over a cup of coffee and discuss the real questions you have about your faith—a friend not afraid to grapple realistically with doubt and willing to admit that they don't have all the answers, but wise and practical in their thinking? In *Coffeehouse Theology* you'll find just such a person: Jim Thomas. The subtitle of the book captures its spirit: *Where Real Questions Get Honest*

Answers. Highly recommended for an overview of the basic issues we all have questions about.

N. T. WRIGHT
The Challenge of Jesus

What could be more important for a Christian than a proper understanding of who Jesus Christ really was? In an age of skepticism and attack from a number of sides, Wright clearly and persuasively argues for the traditional orthodox view of Christ and explains how his mission interacted with the historical environment of his time. A brilliant summary by a theologian who is well respected across ideological lines.

RAVI ZACHARIAS
A Shattered Visage
Can Man Live Without God?

Zacharias has spent years working one of the most challenging mission fields in the world: students at major institutions of higher learning. He has debated and lectured at almost all of our most prestigious universities, bringing the clear message that Jesus Christ is the answer to our human quest for meaning. His books have followed the pattern of his public speaking: clear, intellectually responsible and relevant to the needs and questions of modern men and women. In many ways he wears the mantle once worn by Francis Schaeffer: an evangelist to intellectuals.

Faith and Culture

WENDELL BERRY
What Are People For?
Life Is a Miracle

Berry is one of the most consistently provocative essayists of our time, and his thought is centered in his commitment to faith, simple values and common sense. But he is also not afraid to take aim at some of our most cherished cultural icons. One essay in *What Are People For?*, for example, explains why he refuses to join the computer revolution and still writes longhand texts that are later typed on an old-style typewriter. One of his most recent books, *Life Is a Miracle*, takes dead center aim at the most enduring of modern superstitions, the belief that the answers to our human problems can be found by science. Berry challenges us to see that religion and the arts teach us truths about ourselves that science will never discover. A fine novelist and poet as well, Berry is also listed in chapter eight.

BOB BRINER
Roaring Lambs

Although it is build around a relatively simple thesis, *Roaring Lambs* has exercised a profound impact on a number of well-known Christian musicians, film producers and others in the cultural sphere. Briner argues that Christians who wish to have an impact on their culture should not focus their efforts on creating a separate "Christian" subculture, but should strive for the kind of excellence that will cause their message to be heard outside the confines of the church. A simple but important message.

CHARLES COLSON
Kingdoms in Conflict
The Body
Born Again

A former White House presidential advisor (under Richard Nixon), Colson served time in prison for his role in the Watergate scandal. He became a Christian just shortly before he was convicted and strengthened his faith while in prison. After his release he returned to prison, this time to minister to the needs of imprisoned convicts. His ministry, Prison Fellowship, has changed the lives of countless women and men. The account of his conversion, *Born Again*, is one of the most convincing and compelling conversion stories of the recent times. He has now evolved into one of today's most acute cultural observers. *Kingdoms in Conflict* stakes out a balanced position on Christian involvement in politics, and *The Body* reminds the church of its mission in the modern world. Colson's books are filled with engaging historical accounts, penetrating insights and an unflagging commitment to presenting the gospel message to the twentieth-century mind.

JACQUES ELLUL
The Presence of the Kingdom
Prayer and Modern Man
The Technological Society

Ellul, a French theologian and sociologist, has written a number of books on the relationship between the Christian faith and modern society. His background in sociology affords many brilliant insights into contemporary society, written with the fire and courage of a biblical prophet. *Uncompromising, controversial* and *provocative* are words that come quickly to mind when describing Ellul's work. A helpful introduction to his ideas can be found in a series of interviews published as a book, *In Season, Out of Season.*

DOUG GROOTHUIS
Truth Decay

We no longer live exclusively under the impact of modern rationalistic thought. In the last couple of decades the old-style rationalism has been replaced by a new way of looking at our world and our lives, with new methods of investigating truth. We call this new way of thinking postmodernism. This thorough study by Doug Groothuis is one of the best discussions of the impact that postmodernism has had on our concept of truth and consequently on the Christian faith. A good reminder of the reason why we must keep our eyes and minds open and aware if we are to continue to have an impact on our culture.

OS GUINNESS
The Dust of Death
The American Hour

A student of Francis Schaeffer, Guinness has carried forward and deepened the former's cultural critique. Written in 1973, *The Dust of Death* is a prophetically insightful critique of both the good and the bad that the sixties bequeathed to us. His analysis is probing and foresaw many of the ruin-strewn paths down which our society has strayed. *The American Hour* addresses the place of politics and society in the redemptive plan of God. This book is marked by levelheadedness, bold insight, the avoidance of extreme and simplistic formulas, and a willingness to critique all sides of the current struggle. To be both fair and God-honoring should be the goal of any such critique; Guinness is a model of such in practice. (Chapter seven lists other books by Guinness.)

ALASDAIR MACINTYRE
After Virtue

Although elegantly argued, this book may prove a challenging read for those not schooled in the issues surrounding the philosophy of ethics. Still, it deserves to be read carefully by anyone interested in asking questions about the state of moral discussion in our culture. Meticulously, and with a surprisingly lively tone, MacIntyre demonstrates the difficulty of building a rationalistic basis for morality and calls for a return to the Aristotelian method of Thomas Aquinas. Quite simply one of the most important books of the past decade, *After Virtue* is essential reading for modern Christians asking questions about morality and ethics.

LESSLIE NEWBIGIN
The Gospel in a Pluralist Society

One of the most vexing problems for contemporary Christians is figuring out how to effectively communicate Christianity's truth claims in our secular, relativistic, pluralistic society. Synthesizing the insights of some of today's most profound Christian thinkers, Newbigin provides insightful reflections on how Christians can more effectively communicate their faith to modern men and women. Open-minded yet ultimately orthodox, Newbigin provides in this important book the tools we need for better dialogue and more effective evangelism.

> In a pluralist society such as ours, any confident statement of ultimate belief, any claim to announce the truth about God and his purpose for the world, is liable to be dismissed as ignorant, arrogant, dogmatic. We have no reason to be frightened of this accusation. It itself rests on assumptions which are open to radical criticisms, but which are not criticized because they are part of the reigning plausibility structure. But if we are to meet the criticism . . . we [have] to be faithful bearers of the message entrusted to us.
>
> LESSLIE NEWBIGIN, *The Gospel in a Pluralist Society*

H. RICHARD NIEBUHR
Christ and Culture

Throughout history Christians have continued to struggle with the question of how Christ relates to human culture. How should believers live out their faith in a world that often seems antithetical to the precepts of the gospel? In *Christ and Culture* Niebuhr traces five approaches that believers have taken, from those who have seen culture as the enemy of the gospel to those who see the need of accommodating Christianity to the latest in modern thought. The balance and care of Niebuhr's approach makes this an essential book for anyone thinking about how their faith should be lived out in the world.

MARK NOLL
The Scandal of the Evangelical Mind

"The scandal of the evangelical mind," writes historian Mark Noll, "is that there is not much of an evangelical mind." With these words, Noll launches a scathing critique of the sorry intellectual state of modern evangelicalism, pointing out the many ways that we have departed from our solid intellectual heritage and built a faith based mostly upon feeling and emotion. Noting especially the deleterious effects of this deficiency in Christian thinking about politics and science, Noll challenges evangelicals to strive toward a new intellectual renaissance, one in which the heart and head are wed together to influence our culture with the truth.

FRANCIS SCHAEFFER
The God Who Is There
Escape from Reason
He Is There and He Is Not Silent
How Should We Then Live?

Francis Schaeffer probably did more to challenge modern evangelicals toward deeper thinking about the relationship between Biblical Christianity and the modern intellectual challenges of our time than any other American thinker of the twentieth century. Writing in an engaging way, Schaeffer avoided the typical fundamentalist fears of modern culture and showed how we could engage more constructively with modern philosophy, art, science and other forms of culture. His "trilogy" *(The God Who Is There, Escape from Reason* and *He Is There and He Is Not Silent)* provides the basis for his many subsequent books, including his historical overview *(How Should We Then Live?).* These books have proven indispensable to Christians developing a more thoughtful approach to their faith. (For more of Schaeffer, see chapter three.)

> The problem which confronts us . . . is not how we are to change Christian teaching in order to make it more palatable, for to do that would mean throwing away any chance of giving the real answer . . . rather, it is the problem of how to communicate the gospel so that it is understood.
> FRANCIS SCHAEFFER, *The God Who Is There*

Faith and History

PAUL JOHNSON
Modern Times

Modern Times was an instant classic. It presents a uniquely conservative approach to understanding modern history. Johnson's style is witty, anecdotal and immensely readable, but this does not compromise his thorough and careful historical analysis. This is not the kind of dry-as-dust chronicling of events that many have come to identify with history. Instead, it is history in the grand tradition: wide in scope, relevant and intellectually penetrating. Christian readers will applaud Johnson's contention that the blame for our modern malaise lies squarely on the shoulders of the rise of moral relativism. Many of Johnson's interpretations are reflective of his own conservative and Christian commitments. If you wish to read just one book to help you understand our modern times, you could not do better than Johnson's entertaining and incisive analysis. If you enjoy *Modern Times,* you might explore his *The Birth of the Modern,* which covers the years from 1815 to 1830, or *Intellectuals,* his study of several men whose thinking has shaped our world. Though *Intellectuals* is based a little too much on an ad hominem argument, it does effectively illustrate the weak moral foundations of modernism.

> The modern world began on 29 May 1919 when photographs of a solar eclipse, taken on the island of Principe off West Africa and at Sobral in Brazil, confirmed

> the truth of a new theory of the universe. . . . At the beginning of the 1920s the belief began to circulate, for the first time at a popular level, that there were no longer any absolutes: of time and space, of good and evil, of knowledge, above all of value. Mistakenly but perhaps inevitably, relativity became confused with relativism. PAUL JOHNSON, *Modern Times*

GEORGE MARSDEN
Fundamentalism and American Culture
Reforming Fundamentalism

In these two fascinating and very influential historical studies, Marsden explores the historical underpinnings of the evangelical movement and its continuing struggle with its fundamentalist heritage. He deftly creates memorable portraits of key thinkers and has a knack for capturing the contemporary relevance of the issues at hand. Highly recommended.

MARTIN MARTY
Pilgrims in Their Own Land

The story of religion in the United States is the focus for Marty's excellent historical study, *Pilgrims in Their Own Land*. Through compelling portraits of key thinkers and key moments, Marty has fashioned a narrative with all the excitement of a good historical novel. Part of its value lies in his scope. He has not focused exclusively on Christianity, but has tried to depict all the various religious trends and competing faiths that have flourished in our land, showing the variety of expressions that religious thought and practice have taken.

ROGER E. OLSON
The Story of Christian Theology

By focusing on the lives and personalities of the most important Christian theologians, Olson has found a way to make the struggles of doctrine and dogma fascinating and readable. Though comprehensive in scope, Olson's method makes this book much more enjoyable than the typical textbook on historical theology. It's important to know where we have come from to understand where we are today, and *The Story of Christian Theology* is a great tool for achieving that understanding.

BRUCE SHELLEY
Church History in Plain Language

For anyone who has ever feared that church history was a boring or impenetrable subject, Shelley has created the perfect solution in this readable, down-to-earth church history. Using plain language and not assuming a lot of previous knowledge, Shelley focuses on the key people and key events to provide a basic understanding of the development of the Christian church. This book is an excellent place to begin your study of a fascinating subject. Those who want a more comprehensive study might want to consult Williston Walker's textbook, *A History of the Christian Church*.

Faith and Science

MICHAEL J. BEHE
Darwin's Black Box

Not written with any theological axe to grind, Behe's book delivers a devastating blow to Darwinism by questioning the very foundation of evolutionary theory—evolution at the cellular level. Behe demonstrates, using the concept of irreducible complexity, that evolution appears to be impossible at the microbiological level, thus throwing the entire mechanism of evolution into question. As Behe strives to show, no one has yet been able to suggest a convincing theory for how cellular life evolves. Keeping his argument to the scientific issues, he avoids much reflection on the theological implications of his findings. Although portions of this book are quite technical, Behe is such a clear writer that most of the book can by understood by readers with little scientific background.

FRED HEEREN
Show Me God

Many Christians find themselves feeling threatened by the findings of science, afraid that it will reveal weaknesses in the basis of their faith. But Fred Heeren, writing at a popular level, shows that just the opposite is true: the latest discoveries of science actually point toward the God of the Bible. In this entertaining and well-illustrated volume, Heeren shows the amazing implications of the latest scientific findings. This is a marvelous entry-level book for beginning to explore the complex issue of the relationship between science and faith. Highly recommended.

PHILLIP JOHNSON
Darwin on Trial
Reason in the Balance

Over the years many shamelessly poor critiques of evolution have found their way onto the shelves of Christian bookstores. In such books the evolutionary thinkers have found little in the way of good scientific and logical thinking to challenge their presuppositions. But such is not the case with Phillip Johnson's powerful book *Darwin on Trial.* Armed with careful research and a penetrating logical analysis, Johnson systematically dismantles the key tenets of Darwinism, showing the reliance of this system of thought on some faulty thinking and weak foundational prejudices rather than solid scientific findings. Witty and marvelously compelling, Johnson is the perfect guide for an examination of the flaws of Darwinian evolutionary theory. In *Reason in the Balance* Johnson takes on an even bigger challenge: refuting the philosophy of naturalism that has become the basis for so much of our scientific, philosophical and sociological thinking. As he demonstrates, naturalism is a theory rather than a fact. Both books are important reading for Christians thinking about science and faith.

> When he contemplates the perfidy of those who refuse to believe [in evolution], [Richard] Dawkins can scarcely restrain his fury. "It is absolutely safe to say that, if you meet somebody who claims not to believe in evolution, that person is ignorant, stupid or insane (or wicked, but I'd rather not consider that)." Dawkins went on to explain, by the way, that what he dislikes particularly about creationists is that they are intolerant. PHILLIP JOHNSON, *Darwin on Trial*

HUGH ROSS
The Fingerprint of God
The Creator and the Cosmos

Hugh Ross, an astrophysicist and a Bible scholar, has made it his mission to clear up the questions that arise about the relationship between the findings of science and what the Bible tells us about the creation of the world.

Armed with the latest scientific findings and careful biblical research, Ross helps his readers understand that there is no conflict between the biblical record and scientific fact. Controversial and compelling, Ross demonstrates that a strong commitment to the truth of the Bible doesn't mean you have to be a young earth creationist.

R. C. SPROUL
Not a Chance

The foundation of Darwinism is the idea that life as we know it began not by the hand of a divine Creator, but by the whim of chance. However, as Sproul demonstrates, this concept flies in the face of logic and common sense and has no real intellectual basis. A solid refutation of a philosophical cornerstone of modern evolutionary thinking.

Faith and the Arts

HELEN DE BORCHGRAVE
Journey into Christian Art

Most of the books in this section are more concerned with the literary arts. I guess that's because writers like to write about writing! But this book is a handsomely illustrated guide to the Christian heritage in the visual arts, looking into the lives and beliefs of some of the greatest artists of all time, such as Giotto, Rembrandt, Van Gogh and the Pre-Raphaelites. A solid introduction to our heritage of beauty.

MADELEINE L'ENGLE
Walking on Water

Christians involved in the arts often find themselves in the position of having to defend the spiritual value of their endeavors. A fine novelist, essayist and children's author, L'Engle provides a very personal viewpoint of the issues surrounding faith and the value of the arts. She builds a convincing case for their importance to everyone, especially for the believer. This book has helped many Christians gain new confidence about the worthiness of the arts and freed them to enjoy their richness.

> If my stories are incomprehensible to Jews or Muslims or Taoists, then I have failed as a Christian writer. We do not draw people to Christ by loudly discrediting what they believe, by telling them how wrong they are and how right we are, but by showing them a light that is so lovely that they want with all their hearts to know the source of it. MADELEINE L'ENGLE, *Walking on Water*

C. S. LEWIS
An Experiment in Criticism

In *An Experiment in Criticism* Lewis turns his attention to the value and usefulness of art and literature. As always, he proves to be a stimulating and inspiring guide. With his usual wit and logic, he demonstrates the importance of literature and gives valuable advice on how to become a better reader. Don't miss this little-known gem from one of the twentieth-century's premier Christian thinkers.

FLANNERY O'CONNOR
Mystery and Manners

Generally considered to be one of the finest short story writers of the twentieth century, O'Connor was also a graceful and penetrating essayist. This collection of essays focuses mostly on the relationship between faith and writing. She saw a way of communicating truth in her stories that goes beyond the propagandistic approach that has crippled so much modern Christian storytelling. These provocative essays will give readers deeper insights into what it means to be a Christian writer—or, for that matter, a Christian reader.

HANS ROOKMAAKER
Modern Art and the Death of a Culture
Art Needs No Justification

A protégé of Francis Schaeffer, Rookmaaker was a professional art historian who was interested in the relationship between art and worldview. *Modern Art and the Death of a Culture* makes the argument that much of the ugliness and chaos we see in modern art is a reflection of the nihilistic philosophy of our times. In *Art Needs No Justification*, Rookmaaker argues against the need to find some pragmatic spiritual value in art, thus freeing the

Christian artist for a broader scope of creativity.

> Art . . . has its own meaning as God's creation. . . . Artists need no justification. God called them, gave them talents. We cannot go on without them. So let's help them—in prayer, in encouragement, not with just words but also in deeds according to what we can give. Indeed, what we cannot afford to be without needs no justification. HANS ROOKMAAKER, *Art Needs No Justification*

LELAND RYKEN
The Christian Imagination

This indispensable collection of essays on art, writing and faith contains contributions from such luminary thinkers as C. S. Lewis, T. S. Eliot, Flannery O'Connor, Frank E. Gaebelein and Thomas Howard. A fine primer for beginning to wrestle with the complex issues surrounding faith and art.

STEVE TURNER
Imagine

Turner, a practicing poet and journalist, explores modern evangelical attitudes toward the arts. In this provocative personal essay he chides us for our irrational and unbiblical fear of the arts and calls us to move beyond the goal of creating "alternatives" for our Christian ghetto. He challenges us to produce and support the kind of excellent work that will touch even those who do not embrace our worldview. Further, he asserts that we can find much truth in work produced by non-Christians.

GENE EDWARD VEITH
Reading Between the Lines
State of the Arts
Postmodern Times

Gene Veith has produced several valuable books that help Christians think more clearly about how Christians should respond to the arts. *Reading Between the Lines* addresses the need for becoming more discerning readers. For Veith, that means learning to read with worldviews in mind. Along the way, readers are given an excellent introduction to what literature is and how it functions. *State of the Arts* does the same thing for the visual arts, teaching us how we can appreciate a variety of forms and styles and understand how these can be seen from a Christian perspective. Plus it has a marvelous overview of art history. *Postmodern Times* is a valuable primer to what postmodernism is and how it affects our contemporary culture. Veith is always a writer whose work is worth searching out.

SEVEN

BOOKS TO HELP YOU GROW
IN YOUR SPIRITUAL LIFE

Not long ago a friend handed me a copy of a book on prayer, informing me that it had changed his life. Of course I tore into it with relish, expecting to get some new insights that would strengthen my own devotional life. But by the third chapter I realized that the book wasn't what I'd hoped. Instead, it seemed to me to be a shallow, simplistic rehash of the all the usual niceties about prayer, sprinkled with a little questionable theology and some personal experiences that were, well . . . *pretty strange.*

I've been a Christian long enough to realize that just because something doesn't seem to connect with me, doesn't mean that it might not be of great help to someone else. That book on prayer probably *did* have some positive influence on my friend. But the experience reminded me how difficult it can be to recommend books on the spiritual life.

Christians come from such different backgrounds, with very diverse experiences that have shaped who we are and what we respond to. And God has certainly not created all of us the same. He seems to have implanted different stimuli within each of our souls, meaning that each of us responds to different things. What draws one heart Godward may have a lesser impact on another. This means that my choices for books on the spiritual life may not be the same ones you would make. What is deeply meaningful and life changing to me may cause you to nod in boredom, scratch your head in wonderment or even add me to your prayer list out of concern for my orthodoxy. At the same time, what causes you to respond in worship and adoration may not move me in the least. We each follow our own path.

Yet, I think it's worthwhile to share a list of some of the books that have meant a great deal to me on my own spiritual journey. You might find a kinship with me in my choices, recognizing me as a fellow traveler down the road to a mature faith; then it will certainly be worth hearing about those books I have liked so much. On the other hand, if you don't find any of your favorites here, you may still find some suggestions that could help you expand beyond your usual fare in spiritual reading. And by the way, I'd love to hear about the books that have made an impact on you. I've learned never to be afraid to try something new. If there is one lesson I've learned from reading, it's this: If we keep our minds and hearts open, we'll discover that there is much that others can teach us. And variety does add spice to our spiritual life.

One important note: Many of the very best books on the spiritual life will not be found in this list, which mostly emphasizes contemporary writers. Be sure to spend some time perusing the Christian classics in chapter three to discover some of the greatest treasures of spiritual writing.

JIMMY ABEGG, EDITOR
Ragamuffin Prayers

Abegg has collected the original writings of a number of self-proclaimed "ragamuffins," who share stories, songs, poems and reflections about the struggles, wonder and mystery of prayer. This collection of writings is heartfelt, funny, insightful and painfully honest, mirroring the variety to be found in prayer itself. Among its contributors are Rich Mullins, Brennan Manning, Michael Yaconelli and yours truly. The accompanying photos (by Abegg) have some of the same lyrical beauty and searching honesty as the essays.

NEIL ANDERSON
The Bondage Breaker

Countless books on spiritual warfare are based on specious theology and wild personal experiences. What makes Anderson's book so helpful is its biblical focus and sense of balance between psychological and theological insights. Anderson takes evil seriously but isn't so much focused on some form of exorcism as on changing our perceptions about ourselves. He sees the solution to spiritual bondage in correcting our misconceptions about who we as believers are in Christ. Many have found this book to be extremely helpful in finding victory over compulsive sinful habits and negative thought patterns.

CAROLYN ARENDS
Living the Questions

Life, writes Carolyn Arends, is both a mess and a mystery. If we are to grow as believers, we must accept this hard truth and capture a fresh glimpse of how God guides us gently through all our questions and doubts. Honest, humorous, searching and lyrical, Arends writes of moments from her own spiritual journey that cast light on the spiritual path that each of us must walk. Arends's celebration of "the preposterous optimism I've come to recognize as faith" makes for a marvelous reading experience.

> Once I entered a little way into the Mystery, there was no going back. I could no longer list all the things I did not understand about God as threats to my faith—instead, they became the primary evidence that God was, in fact, God . . . and that I was, in fact, not. The Divine Frustration was a terrible strain. But it was also an indication that something infinite really existed, something my finite three-and-a-half pounds of brain could only know in part, like peering through a dark glass at a reality too intense to be seen safely with the naked human eye.
>
> CAROLYN ARENDS, *Living the Questions*

JOHN BAILLIE
A Diary of Private Prayer

This collection of a month's worth of prayers (one for each morning and one for each evening) has become a cherished part of the devotional lives of many believers. Baillie's prayers are literate, heart-searching and universal in scope. Spend a month with John Baillie to inspire your own life of prayer.

BOB BENSON SR. AND MICHAEL W. BENSON
Disciplines for the Inner Life

I can't say enough about how valuable this book has been to my own spiritual journey. This year-long guide to a deeper spiritual life is a marvelous handbook for every Christian. It includes a Scripture passage and an insightful reading from a classical or contemporary writer for each day of the year, plus prayers and a hymn for each week. The readings and prayers are grouped by key themes of the spiritual life: prayer, confession, discipline, humility, compassion, guidance and so on. Having this much wisdom distilled in one place makes this one of the very best tools for spiritual growth of which I know. Dedicate a year to working through it, and it will change you for the rest of your life.

ROBERT BENSON
Living Prayer

In *Living Prayer* Benson has written the kind of book that makes the contemplative approach to prayer—an approach many Christians believe is out of reach for their own spiritual lives—practical enough to work into anyone's lifestyle. With an honesty based on his personal successes and failures, Benson shares his own experiences and shows readers how to make prayer a part of the fabric of their daily existence. One of my favorite books on prayer.

DONALD BLOESCH
The Crisis of Piety
The Struggle of Prayer

When it comes to our spirituality, we must understand why we have embraced the practices and convictions we hold dear. In these two books eminent theologian Donald Bloesch constructs a solid theological underpinning for a balanced and biblical understanding of the spiritual life and the centrality of prayer. Bloesch has obviously read widely and thought deeply, trying to take the best from both the contemplative and prophetic traditions. The resulting books are filled with brilliant and balanced insights. Highly recommended, as is just about anything Bloesch has written.

DIETRICH BONHOEFFER
Life Together

This slim volume is based on lectures Bonhoeffer gave to seminarians of the Confessing Church (a group of believers opposed to Hitler) during the dark days of Nazi rule in Germany. The book deals with both individual spiritual growth and how we can come together more effectively as a community of believers. A classic definitely not to be missed! (Other Bonhoeffer titles are listed in chapter three.)

CHARLES COLSON
Loving God

It's hard to think of a book that better summarizes what it means to be a Christian than Colson's *Loving God*. Through stories both contemporary and historical, he explains in a clear and interesting manner what the life of faith is all about. If you are interested in Colson's own journey toward faith, read his moving autobiography, *Born Again*. (Other Colson titles are listed in chapter six.)

ANNIE DILLARD
A Pilgrim at Tinker Creek
Teaching a Stone to Talk

Dillard writes prose that is as dense and lovely as poetry. Her books are full of achingly beautiful writing that reflects on the ways of God as evidenced in nature. She is an observer as acute as Thoreau, but with an underlying commitment to God's superintendence over the natural order. She is a mystic whose words take wing and soar; our hearts and minds cannot help but follow.

> It is difficult to undo our own damage, and to recall to our presence that which we have asked to leave. It is hard to desecrate a grove and change your mind. The very holy mountains are keeping mum. We doused the burning bush and cannot rekindle it; we are lighting matches in vain under every green tree.
>
> What have we been doing all these centuries but trying to call God back to the mountain, or, failing that, raise a peep out of anything that isn't us? What is the difference between a cathedral and a physics lab? Are they not both saying: Hello! ANNIE DILLARD, *A Pilgrim at Tinker Creek*

JOHN ELDREDGE

The Sacred Romance (with Brent Curtis)
The Journey of Desire

Eldredge writes wonderfully on the role that desire plays in the spiritual life. He shows God to be the Great Lover, who has placed within our hearts desires that only he can fulfill. If we follow the clues of beauty and passion, they will ultimately lead us to the One who wishes to capture us with his love. These are courageous books that call us to move beyond some of our usual evangelical preoccupations, thinking more deeply and feeling more passionately as we seek the end of all our desires.

RICHARD FOSTER

Celebration of Discipline
Prayer: The Heart's True Home
Streams of Living Water

I have talked to many people who would concur with me, based on their own experience, that *Celebration of Discipline* is literally a life-changing book. In this book Foster discusses the necessity for discipline in the Christian life through the practice of prayer, meditation, fasting, worship, service and other spiritual disciplines. For me the book opened up a whole new appreciation for the classics on spirituality and added depth and focus to my spiritual life. Foster's book on prayer is equally powerful and one of the rare books on the subject that really does drive readers joyfully to their knees. *Streams of Living Water* examines the various traditions of the Christian faith and demonstrates that they all have powerful lessons to teach toward the goal of a more balanced faith.

Finally, for those interested in sampling some of the best spiritual writing from the classics, try Foster's two anthologies of short selections from some of the best spiritual writers: *Devotional Classics* and *Spiritual Classics*.

> Superficiality is the curse of our age. The doctrine of instant satisfaction is a primary spiritual problem. The desperate need today is not for a greater number of intelligent people, or gifted people, but for deep people.
>
> The classical disciplines of the spiritual life call us to move beyond surface living into the depths. They invite us to explore the inner caverns of the spiritual realm. They urge us to be the answer to a hollow world. . . .

Psalm 42:7 reads "Deep calls to deep." Perhaps somewhere in the subterranean chambers of your life you have heard the call to deeper, fuller living. You have become weary of frothy experiences and shallow teaching. Every now and then you have caught glimpses, hints of something more than you have known. Inwardly you long to launch out into the deep.

RICHARD FOSTER, *Celebration of Discipline*

GARRY FRIESEN
Decision Making and the Will of God

Many Christians struggle with how they can know God's will for them in both the big and small decisions of life. In *Decision Making and the Will of God*, Friesen offers a sane, balanced, biblical view of this critical question. There are no simple answers here, but good guidance for how to choose God's best for our lives.

KEN GIRE
Windows of the Soul

In *Windows of the Soul* Gire invites us to experience God in new ways, learning to "look with more than just our eyes and listen with more than just our ears." He points to those unexpected places where, if we are attentive, we might hear the voice of God, for example, in stories, art, poetry, movies, memories and tears. As with most of Gire's books, this one is warm in tone and beautiful in execution.

TERRY GLASPEY
A Time for Prayer
The Journey of Prayer
The Joy of Prayer
The Experience of Prayer

Several years ago I set out to see what I could learn about prayer from the classic books and writers of the Christian tradition. This series of four small books is the result of that research. I've gathered together the best thoughts on virtually every area of prayer (confession, supplication, intercession, why God doesn't seem to answer, spiritual warfare and much more) from some of the greatest Christian writers of all time (Augustine, C. S. Lewis, Luther,

Calvin, Merton, Spurgeon and many others). The result is a readable and practical distillation of the wisdom of the ages on prayer. I've also included some of my favorite classic prayers.

EMILIE GRIFFIN
Clinging

This might be the most poetic little meditation you'll ever read on prayer, but it loses none of its practical power in its lyrical expression. *Clinging*'s emphasis lies in dealing with prayer not as something to think about, but as an experience to be lived firsthand. I also heartily recommend Griffin's study of the process of conversion entitled *Turning*.

OS GUINNESS
God in the Dark (formerly *In Two Minds*)
When No One Sees
Steering Through Chaos

It's hard to think of a more consistently engaging contemporary writer than Os Guinness. The breadth of his reading is staggering, and the depth of his insight is remarkable. He is one of those rare writers whose every book is worth exploring. *God in the Dark* is a realistic look at the problem of doubt in the spiritual life. Guinness not only explores the various causes of doubt, but he also shows how it can be used to strengthen our commitment of faith. It is an important book on an important subject and deserves classic status. The other two volumes listed above look at the importance of strong personal character *(When No One Sees)* and how to overcome the seven deadly vices *(Steering Through Chaos)*. They use the insights of classic literature (selections from fiction by Hawthorne, Tolstoy, William Golding, Victor Hugo and others) and modern essayists (such as C. S. Lewis, Robert Coles and Frederick Buechner) to explore how we can make changes in the way we live our lives.

ABRAHAM HESCHEL
I Asked for Wonder

One of my favorite writers on the spiritual life, Heschel is a Jewish theologian whose insights deserve to be meditated upon by Christians. He combines profundity with simplicity and has an amazing gift for metaphors and images that help us better understand the spiritual life and how we stand before God. This particular volume is a collection of his aphorisms and spiritual wisdom, drawn from a variety of his books. If you enjoy it, you might also want to explore *Man's Quest for God.*

> Prayer is no panacea, no substitute for action. It is, rather, like a beam thrown from a flashlight before us into the darkness. It is in this light that we who grope, stumble, and climb, discover where we stand, what surrounds us, and the course we should choose. Prayer makes visible the right, and reveals what is hampering and false. In its radiance, we behold the worth of our efforts, the range of our hopes, and the meaning of our deeds. ABRAHAM HESCHEL, *I Asked for Wonder*

JAMES HOUSTON
The Transforming Friendship
The Heart's Desire

Houston is a student of the great spiritual writers of the past and a man whose humility and good sense are evident on every page of his writing. He is a contemplative spirit who is solidly evangelical in his convictions and theology. *Transforming Friendship* is his insightful look at prayer; *The Heart's Desire* is his exploration of the reality that only relationship with God can bring true personal fulfillment.

BILL HYBELS
Too Busy Not to Pray

One of the things that tends to keep us from praying is the perception that we are simply too busy to pray. But as Hybels reminds us, we are "too busy not to pray." Hybels discovered the hard truth that prayer doesn't happen very effectively on the run. He offers practical advice on how we can slow down our lives and make room for the highest priority: developing our relationship with God. A good basic primer on prayer that is honest about the difficulties involved.

MORTON KELSEY
Encounter with God

Kelsey is a prolific writer on the spiritual life who sometimes seems a bit too attached to Jungian psychology for my personal taste. Still, his books are solidly researched and interesting attempts to make faith reasonable and psychologically compelling for the modern reader. *Encounter with God*, one of his earliest books, is still my favorite. It provides a well-argued case for the reality of the supernatural realm, based on the findings of psychology, science and theology. If read with some discernment, later books such as *The Other Side of Silence* (a study of meditation) and *Companions on the Inner Way* also have much to offer.

SUE MONK KIDD
When the Heart Waits

We live in a time nourished mostly by fast-food spirituality and quick-fix answers, always in a hurry to find simple solutions for our problems. But Kidd suggests a different path: learning the spiritual discipline of waiting. If we are willing to take the slow and gradual path, which will involve the art of active waiting, God can help us learn to overcome our false selves (constructed to fulfill the expectations of others) and find our truest self in obedience to his vocation for our lives. If you feel too harried to concentrate on your spiritual life, take my advice: slow down and take the time to digest this fine book. Unfortunately, her later books veer into serious theological heresies and must be read with a great deal of discernment.

PETER KREEFT
Heaven: The Heart's Deepest Longing
Making Sense Out of Suffering

Peter Kreeft is a philosophy professor with a unique knack for making even the most complex philosophical and theological ideas accessible to the common reader. The biggest influence on Kreeft is obviously C. S. Lewis, on whose work he has penned three books. This influence shows clearly in Kreeft's wonderful mix of intellectual and intuitive argumentation. His apologetical emphasis is certainly welcome in our confusing modern times, and he is a popularizer of the highest order. *Heaven: The Heart's Deepest Longing* uses Lewis's argument about longing as the basis for a marvelous study of heaven as the place all our hearts long for. *Making Sense Out of Suffering* is one of the most balanced and satisfying attempts to answer that most difficult of questions: why would a good God allow so much suffering in his world? (Other books by Kreeft are listed in chapter six.)

ANNE LAMOTT
Traveling Mercies

This *New York Times* bestseller is a spiritual memoir by a leading contemporary novelist. She brings a breath of fresh air to contemporary religious writing. Lamott shows herself a master of self-deprecating humor as she writes of her own spiritual journey toward faith with a disarming honesty and—for a religious book—very "earthy" vocabulary. Once you've glimpsed faith through Anne Lamott's eyes, you'll never look at things quite the same way again.

MADELEINE L'ENGLE
A Circle of Quiet

A Circle of Quiet is the first in a series of journals (The Crosswicks Journal) that reflect on the events of L'Engle's life, the surprising motions of grace, and the mystery of love and creativity. The other books in the series, definitely worth exploring, are *The Summer of the Great-Grandmother, The Irrational Season* and *Two-Part Invention*. Also, don't miss her wonderfully personal book on the relationship between faith and art, *Walking on Water*.

C. S. LEWIS
Mere Christianity
Letters to Malcolm: Chiefly on Prayer
The Screwtape Letters

Mere Christianity is the only book I've recommended in three categories: spirituality, Christian thinking and classics. That says something about the scope and value of this collection of essays, once given as wartime radio lectures. When I was a young believer this book had an incredible impact on my spiritual life. I've returned to it time and again over the years, only to find more fresh insight for my personal growth. I've tried to avoid the term *must-read* in this book, but *Mere Christianity* deserves that categorization. *Letters to Malcolm* is Lewis's examination of prayer, and it is, predictably, filled with wisdom, humor, depth and practical good sense. *The Screwtape Letters* is a clever look at the spiritual life through the eyes of a senior devil who is giving advice to a junior devil on the ins and outs of temptation. Particularly valuable are its chapters on the ups and downs of the spiritual life, its "peaks and valleys," and the necessity to live at a deeper level than our religious feelings. For a glimpse of Lewis's life and teaching, see my book *Not a Tame Lion: The Spiritual Legacy of C. S. Lewis.* (Lewis titles are also listed in chapters three and six.)

MAX LUCADO
No Wonder They Call Him Savior

Max Lucado has earned a sizable reading audience with his elegantly simple storytelling that manages to be inspiring without being preachy. His "you are there" retellings of Bible stories are especially effective.

BRENNAN MANNING
Lion and Lamb
The Ragamuffin Gospel

We talk a lot about grace in modern evangelical circles, but often our actions and attitudes show a greater indebtedness to legalistic thinking. What makes Manning's writing so powerful is that he takes the message of God's love at face value and proposes that we accept the radical conclusions of this belief at face value. When we do, it flies in the face of some of our cherished religious notions, but it also imparts to us the freedom to live in honesty as God's beloved children. We may be ragamuffins, still struggling with sin and darkness, but we are loved, accepted and forgiven. His message boils down to this: there is nothing we can do to make God love us more, and there is nothing we can do to make God love us any less. Manning seems to enjoy tweaking our sense of religious propriety and imparting a fresh vision of God's accepting love.

> When I get honest, I admit that I am a bundle of paradoxes. I believe and I doubt, I hope and I get discouraged, I love and I hate, I feel bad about feeling good, I feel guilty about not feeling guilty. I am trusting and suspicious. I am honest and I still play games. Aristotle said I am a rational animal; I say I am an angel with an incredible capacity for beer. . . .
>
> To live by grace means to acknowledge my whole life's story, the light side and the dark. In admitting my shadow side, I learn who I am and what God's

grace means. As Thomas Merton put it, "A saint is not someone who is good but who experiences the goodness of God."
BRENNAN MANNING, *The Ragamuffin Gospel*

THOMAS MERTON
Contemplative Prayer
Thoughts in Solitude

Although rooted in the Catholic tradition of spirituality, Merton's books cross the boundary between Catholic and Protestant, appealing to almost anyone desiring to find more spiritual depth in their life. These two volumes by the immensely prolific writer are a good sampling of what Merton has to offer the reader in his many books: spiritual depth, psychological understanding and a sense of realism about what it means to be a human being. (Other Merton titles are listed in chapter three.)

HENRI NOUWEN
The Way of the Heart
Genesee Diary
Making All Things New
The Return of the Prodigal Son

One of the premier modern writers about the spiritual life, Nouwen was a Catholic whose work touches those from all denominational and confessional groups due to its evocation of simple and honest devotion. *The Way of the Heart,* a series of devotional meditations on the lives of the desert fathers, emphasizes the need to make solitude and inner silence a part of our spiritual maturation. *Genesee Diary* records Nouwen's experiences living for an extended period of time with the monks in the Genesee monastery. It provides an honest and inspiring view of the life of the cloister. *Making All Things New* is an examination of what it means to live a spiritual life. Inspired by his meditations on a famous painting by Rembrandt, *The Return of the Prodigal Son* is a soul-searching and healing look at the heart of God and his inexhaustible love for his children. Nouwen's entire body of work is definitely one of the twentieth century's most nourishing spiritual treasures. All of his many books repay close reading.

EUGENE PETERSON
A Long Obedience in the Same Direction

In the midst of an evangelical subculture that sometimes seems to have as its goal making it increasingly easier to be a Christian, Peterson calls us to a deeper life of faith, one that is not based on a quick fix but on a "long obedience." In this book he shows us, through a study of the book of Psalms, how we can commit ourselves to true discipleship, following God for the long haul. It is a bracing challenge, delivered with Peterson's characteristically clear and vigorous writing. Other fine Eugene Peterson titles include *Traveling Light, Reversed Thunder* and *Answering God*. He is also the translator of *The Message*, a recent Bible version that makes the Scriptures sing with vibrant new life.

J. B. PHILLIPS
Your God Is Too Small

The root cause of many spiritual problems is that we have an inadequate conception of who God is. In this sparkling little volume, Phillips uses his abundant wit to take aim at our false and insufficient views of God, challenging us to see God in his fullness rather than forcing on him our own unworthy mental pictures. When we see God as he is, rather than consigning him to a comfortable little box of our own making, we will find the strength to commit ourselves to him wholeheartedly and live out our lives as he intended.

REBECCA MANLEY PIPPERT
Out of the Saltshaker

"Christians and non-Christians have something in common," writes Rebecca Pippert. "We're both uptight about evangelism." And this isn't very surprising, considering the fact that we've often been trained to witness as though we were hawking some new product that could improve people's lives. Pippert moves past this sales-techniques approach to show how we can share our faith naturally, in a way that really communicates with our modern neighbors and friends. Her personal stories and winsome insights can help us feel more relaxed and enthusiastic about sharing the good news.

LEWIS SMEDES
Forgive and Forget

Few things hamper our spiritual lives as much as long-held bitterness and resentment. Smedes warns us of the spiritual dangers of unforgiveness and provides practical steps we can take to learn to forgive those who have hurt us. Putting this message into practice will help us experience the freedom that comes in forgiving as we have been forgiven.

BILLY SPRAGUE
Ice Cream as a Clue to the Meaning of the Universe
Letter to a Grieving Heart

In *Ice Cream,* a collection of whimsical and honest reflections, Sprague offers a fresh window through which to see our world. Writing from his own experiences, Sprague shares openly and movingly about his own struggles with pain, loss and loneliness, and about how he has found meaning in the unquenchable longing God has placed in every soul. This is a delightful book that is honest about the pain and chaos that surrounds us and is within us, but is also filled with hope and a sense of wonder at the beauty of our daily lives. Because it so artfully avoids all the clichés of most Christian writing, this is one of those rare books that you can give to a nonbeliever, confident that it can slip past the defenses they have built against the Christian faith. *Letter to a Grieving Heart* is the perfect little book to give someone who has recently experienced the death of a loved one. With refreshing honesty and gently offered advice, Sprague shares from his own experience and offers a hand to hold on the journey back to embracing life.

CORRIE TEN BOOM
The Hiding Place

One of the most powerful spiritual memoirs of the twentieth century. In this fine book, Ten Boom tells the story of her imprisonment (along with her saintly sister) in a Nazi concentration camp for the crime of helping her family hide endangered Jews. This powerful story of courage, heroism, spiritual strength and forgiveness will not soon be forgotten by those who read it. The prequel *(In My Father's House)* and the sequel *(Tramp for the Lord)* to this book are also enjoyable and inspiring.

GARY THOMAS
Seeking the Face of God
Sacred Pathways

In a series of books that show his deep indebtedness to classic devotional writing, Thomas proves himself a worthy successor to the great spiritual writers. When I first read *Seeking the Face of God*, I used up nearly all the ink in my pen, marking numerous memorable passages and worthy insights. It is one of the very best summations of the various aspects of the spiritual life that I have ever read, filled with much food for thought and with abundant practical steps that will deepen the spirituality of the reader. Although *Seeking* is still my favorite of his writings, his other books are also worth exploring. Especially worthwhile is *Sacred Pathways*, which helps readers determine what kind of spiritual path is best for them to travel and how to balance the strengths and weaknesses of their personal approach by learning from those with differing emphases to their spirituality. Practical, biblical and rooted in the Christian classics, Thomas's books are worthy of your attention.

A. W. TOZER
The Pursuit of God

Tozer manages to break out of the cliché-ridden lingo that characterizes much of the evangelical writing on the spiritual life. What emerges is a book notable for its depth of insight into the human spirit and for the single-hearted passion of its author for the Savior. Magnificent! (This book is also listed in chapter three.)

SHELDON VANAUKEN
A Severe Mercy

In a true-life love story that is at once deeply passionate and spiritually uplifting, Vanauken relates the story of his own marriage. *A Severe Mercy* is intoxicatingly romantic, deeply tragic and ultimately filled with hope and wonder. Vanauken and Davy built a relationship like few you will ever read of, only to have it torn from them by her early death of an incurable illness. Readers will find themselves challenged to deepen their own marriages but warned against the danger of letting such relationships come between them and God. Readers will also find themselves challenged to live the life that God has given them with expectancy and wonder, cherishing every precious moment.

BOB WELCH
A Father for All Seasons
Where Roots Grow Deep

A newspaper reporter and columnist by trade, Welch is a masterful storyteller. He shares stories from his own life and those whom he has met during his years with a daily city paper to help us gain a deeper realization about the place our families and our past have in our lives. His theme is the nurturing love of families, and I know of no one who writes of this subject in a more moving manner. Welch will often make you laugh, but you should also have a box of tissues handy.

DALLAS WILLARD
The Spirit of the Disciplines
The Divine Conspiracy

An essential companion to Richard Foster's books, *The Spirit of the Disciplines* was written by one of his close friends. A philosopher and theologian, Willard gives a biblical and theological justification for the centrality of the spiritual disciplines in the life of the growing believer. It is a profound look at the methods God uses to change our lives. Salvation, asserts Willard, is not only forgiveness of sins but also transformation. *The Divine Conspiracy*, a later book, is a brilliant study of the meaning of our existence and how we can experience the reality of God on a day-by-day basis, with a focus on what it means to be a disciple of Jesus Christ. Richard Foster calls *The Divine Conspiracy* "the book I have been searching for all my life." One would be hard-pressed to argue with his assessment of the book's importance.

MICHAEL YACONELLI
Dangerous Wonder

In this marvelous little book, Yaconelli acknowledges the child within us all and challenges us not to lose the childlike sense of wonder and the willingness to take risks that we had at an earlier age. If you have been raised in the tradition of a stuffy, overly responsible approach to your Christian life, you'll find a bracing tonic in Yaconelli's call to let your spirit soar with wild abandon, irresponsible passion and naive grace. As Donald McCullough said of this book, "I felt my spirit loosen its tie, kick off its shoes, and run out to play in the sunshine of God's grace." I felt the same way.

> Immorality is much more than adultery and dishonesty; it is living drab, colorless, dreary, stale, unimaginative lives. The greatest enemy of Christianity may be people who say they believe in Jesus but who are no longer astonished and amazed. Jesus came to rescue us from listlessness as well as lostness; He came to save us from flat souls as well as corrupted souls. He came to save us from dullness. . . .
>
> Somewhere along the way we had the child chased out of us. Our childlikeness is usually snuffed out by people who tell us what we can't do. They are dream stealers. MICHAEL YACONELLI, *Dangerous Wonder*

PHILIP YANCEY
Disappointment with God
The Jesus I Never Knew
Reaching for the Invisible God

Although a prolific writer, Yancey has yet to write a book that isn't well worth reading. He is one of those rare writers for whom popularity (his books have consistently been bestsellers) and quality come together. One of the most consistently important voices of modern evangelicalism, Yancey seems to be able to tweak our cherished notions in a way that no other religious writer seems to get away with. He can do this because his work is grounded in brilliant observational skills, wide reading and a sense of balance between the secular and sacred spheres of our lives. Also, he is willing to ask the hard questions, the ones we all ask in the depths of our hearts. And he doesn't settle for simple, pat answers but acknowledges the struggles. Finally, he is a marvelous communicator, always seeming to find just the right words to communicate clearly and memorably.

Disappointment with God is a very candid reflection on why God sometimes seems to be so removed from meeting our deepest emotional needs and how to deal with the sense of anger and frustration we can feel toward him. *The Jesus I Never Knew* challenges us to look beyond our Sunday-school images of Christ and gain a deeper understanding of his person and purpose. *Reaching for the Invisible God* asks the important question, How can we have a real relationship with someone we cannot see, hear or touch? Of course, if you enjoy these three, don't stop there. *Where Is God When It Hurts?, What's So Amazing About Grace?* and *The Bible Jesus Read* are all excellent books as well.

EIGHT

CONTEMPORARY FICTION

Many Christians are a bit nervous about modern fiction, based as it often is on themes that can be shocking or discomforting. Contemporary novels are often littered with profanity and coarse language. Sometimes they contain a negative view of Christians or the Christian faith. It isn't surprising, then, that some Christians would rather devote themselves to more "uplifting" and "inspirational" reading, books where good always triumphs and we are given fictionalized models for godly living.

There is, of course, nothing wrong with a book that is inspiring or brings a satisfied smile to your face. Everyone enjoys a happy ending. But the serious novel cannot limit itself to themes that have this kind of uplifting effect on our psyche. We also need books that make us think, that cause us to face our inner demons or that shock us out of complacency. That is what the best of modern literature can do for us. By showing us all of life—even the seedy side—it helps us come to terms with the darkness and sin within ourselves and within our society.

We cannot write honestly about what it means to be a human being without taking into account the reality of human sinfulness. The human experience is not all sweetness and light, with a happy ending to wrap everything up nicely. Instead, we struggle with things like lust, greed, hatred, blasphemy, loss, violence and revenge. If we do not speak of such things in our fiction, we are not telling the whole story about what it means to be a human being. We may not cherish such aspects—they may in fact be difficult for us to look at or read about—but they are the lived realities of human existence.

In the list of books that follows, you'll find a variety of reading experiences. Some of these novels are inspiring, spiritually uplifting and warmhearted. Others are darker in tone, dealing honestly with human struggles and the effects of human fallenness. You'll discover some books that have strong language and profanity or deal openly with issues like human sexuality, racism, violence and loss of faith. If they make you squirm a bit, that is part of their intent.

Some will argue that it is not spiritually healthy to expose yourself to such writing. And ultimately, everybody has to decide for themselves how much unsettling reality they can take and what they will choose to expose themselves to. Each must determine his or her own idea of what is appropriate. I only venture to suggest that we not draw the line in such a way as to set up a bulwark against reality. We all need to be challenged and confronted sometimes by the darker truths of what it means to be a human being.

One of the things that reading modern novels does for us is help us to better understand our friends, neighbors and acquaintances who are not believers. It reminds us of the issues that are paramount in their hearts and minds, the questions they are asking. We need to have enough compassion to learn the questions of our own time. Each age asks different questions about human identity, meaning and purpose. The best of our modern novelists are articulating these questions. By reading them we find a window into the mental, emotional and spiritual struggles of our own time. We cannot afford to be ignorant of how our contemporaries think if we are to make the good news of the gospel relevant and clear to them. While many modern writers may have no answers for the questions they pose, we can use their work to point others to the answers found in the purposes of God.

So be challenged and uplifted, discomforted and entertained by some of the best contemporary writers. Read with discernment but with an open mind. You'll discover some life-changing reading below.

CHINUA ACHEBE
Things Fall Apart

Achebe established himself as the premier African novelist of our time with this tragic tale of the life of a proud man seeking his rightful place in his tribal world. It has the gravity of a classical Greek tragedy but is written with an economy of words and subtle irony. It demonstrates, at the same time, both the disruptive and the redemptive effect of the missionaries who bring the gospel to a people already entrenched in their own religious traditions.

MARGARET ATWOOD
The Handmaid's Tale

A chilling futuristic novel about a society in which the role of women has been reduced to their function as housekeepers and childbearers. To Atwood's credit, what could have become a shrill feminist tract is instead well-imagined and humane. She exposes the potential dangers of a society that, in seeking the highest moral standards, has lost its way, descending into misogyny and fascism.

SAUL BELLOW
The Adventures of Augie March
Herzog
Mr. Sammler's Planet
Humboldt's Gift

One of the best living novelists in the world today, the Canadian Saul Bellow writes novels that are compulsively readable but filled with intellectual substance. Though his books are a feast for the mind, full of provocative ideas and trenchant cultural analysis, they breathe with vibrant life because of his ability to create wonderfully sympathetic and memorable characters. Bellow's consistent theme is the growth of the soul, our search to make sense of our lives and find relationships that will nourish and bring meaning in the midst of all the struggles and trials of life. In many ways, Bellow seems to me to be the closest living equivalent to the richness of the tradition of Russian novelists.

> I am an American, Chicago born—Chicago, that somber city—and go at things as I have taught myself, free-style, and will make the record in my own way: first to knock, first admitted; sometimes an innocent knock, sometimes a not so innocent. But a man's character is his fate, says Heraclitus, and in the end there isn't any way to disguise the nature of the knocks by acoustical work on the door or gloving the knuckles.
>
> SAUL BELLOW, *The Adventures of Augie March*

WENDELL BERRY
Jayber Crow

This novel is the latest (at the time of my writing) and probably most fully realized of Berry's series of novels and short stories about the fictional town of Port William, Kentucky. Berry's inimitable style catches the flavor of a life lived at a slower and more thoughtful pace, and he draws characters that seem as real as your friends and neighbors. From the stance of his faith commitment, Berry calls us to a simpler and more authentic way of living. Written in first person, *Jayber Crow* tells the story of an orphaned child who sets out to be a minister, but whose questions end up causing him to cut short his seminary education and settle down as a barber in Port William. There, standing in back of his barber chair and listening to the stories of his customers, he begins to find some of the answers that have eluded him for so long. Other novels and short story collections in this series include *Nathan Coulter, The Memory of Old Jack, Wild Birds, Remembering, Fidelity, Watch with Me* and *A World Lost.*

JORGE LUIS BORGES
Labyrinths
Dream Tigers

Borges's favorite genre was the very short story. Few of them stretch beyond a handful of pages. But he provides much to think about in very few words. Rather than participating in the traditional narrative tradition, his stories are fascinating and curious intellectual puzzles. Defying description, they must simply be experienced to be appreciated. There is really no other reading experience quite like Borges's highly original work.

FREDERICK BUECHNER
The Book of Bebb
Godric
Telling the Truth: The Gospel as Comedy, Tragedy, and Fairy Tale

A brilliant sense of humor and the aptitude to see the divine at work in the mundane circumstances of daily life gives Buechner's fiction and nonfiction the ability not only to move readers deeply but also to help them see more acutely into their own lives. This sensitivity, wedded with an unflinching honesty about all of our doubts and questions concerning the life of faith, lifts his work above the propagandistic approach of much religious writing. It is hard to pick the best of his work, for he maintains a high degree of quality throughout. *Telling the Truth* demonstrates his ability as an essayist. The four novels collected in *The Book of Bebb* (about a religious con man— or is he some kind of saint?) and the artful lyrical retelling of the life of a medieval monk *(Godric)* show Buechner to be among our finest modern novelists. Also very worthwhile are his "theological dictionary," *Wishful Thinking*, and the series of memoirs beginning with *The Sacred Journey.* Actually, nearly everything from Buechner's pen is worth reading.

> "Praise, praise!" I croak. Praise God for all that's holy, cold, and dark. Praise him for all we lose, for all the river of years bears off. Praise him for stillness in the wake of pain. Praise him for emptiness. And as you race to spill into the sea, praise him yourself, old Wear. Praise him for dying and the peace of death.
>
> In the little church I built of wood for Mary, I hollowed out a place for him. Perkin brings him by the pail and pours him in. Now that I can hardly walk, I crawl to meet him there. He takes me in his chilly lap to wash me of my sins. Or I kneel down beside him till within his depths I see a star.
>
> Sometimes this star is still. Sometimes she dances. She is Mary's star. Within that little pool of Wear she winks at me. I wink at her. The secret that we share I cannot tell in full. But this much I will tell. What's lost is nothing to what's found, and all the death that ever was, set next to life, would scarcely fill a cup.
> FREDERICK BUECHNER, *Godric*

A. S. BYATT
Possession: A Romance

As is the case with all her novels, Byatt's *Possession* is endlessly inventive and shows the mark of her scholarship and love of research. In this novel two contemporary scholars discover a trail of evidence about a passionate love affair between two esteemed Romantic poets that will lead to a reexamination of their life and work. In the process, they learn something about themselves and about the nature of love and duty. Byatt's brilliance is seen in the fact that she has recreated the poetry of the two poets, as well as their letters and diaries, in a way that is entirely convincing. These sections read as though they are authentic nineteenth century artifacts. But it is her modern tale that keeps us turning pages.

WILL CAMPBELL
Brother to a Dragonfly

The autobiography of an early civil rights leader in the Deep South. By turns this book is uproariously funny in its salty language and down-home humor, and piercingly prophetic. His definition of *grace*—"we're all bastards, but God loves us anyway"—mirrors Campbell's courageous stand for the dignity of all God's children and serves as a reminder of how easy it is for the church to ride the wave of culture and fail to take a stand on important issues of justice. Will Campbell shows us that to be a Christian is to be fully human and to be committed to respecting the humanity of all people.

FRANK CONROY
Body and Soul

A completely enchanting novel about the power of music. Claude is a Mozart-like child prodigy, born into poverty and a broken home (his mother drives a cab in New York at night to make ends meet), but with a special gift for music. The novel chronicles the struggles he faces as he climbs to a place of esteem within the musical community and the people who help him along the way. His impoverished roots shadow him in this glitzy world, as does his sense of right and wrong. Tender and beautifully told, it is peopled with the kind of characters the reader comes to care about.

PAT CONROY
The Prince of Tides

A sprawling novel spanning forty years in the life of Tom Wingo and his troubled twin sister, Savannah, both marked by their dark and violent past. Dramatic, funny and eloquent by turns, Conroy has fashioned a compulsively readable page-turner with strong literary qualities. Not to be missed.

DOUGLAS COUPLAND
Generation X
Life After God
Microserfs

Coupland, who coined the phrase "generation X," has become the literary chronicler of his generation. With his sardonic humor and keen power of observation, he has captured the ennui and rootlessness of his peers to perfection. Stylistically, he might be compared to Kurt Vonnegut, always ready to entertain and instruct with his witty off-the-point asides and buoyant sense of humor. *Life After God* is especially interesting for its examination of the void created in our lives when God is considered irrelevant. And Coupland seems to stumble fairly close to the solution for that problem.

MICHAEL CUNNINGHAM
The Hours

A Pulitzer Prize-winning novel that intertwines three story lines: an ordinary but dissatisfied middle-class housewife, a gay poet dying of AIDS and the English novelist Virginia Woolf. Cunningham treats each of his characters with dignity and compassion, making us care deeply about their lives. He also writes quite beautifully and has crafted a marvelous read.

ROBERTSON DAVIES
The Rebel Angels
What's Bred in the Bone
The Lyre of Orpheus

Canadian novelist and playwright Robertson Davies dazzles with his energetic writing, his love for the unusual and uncanny (ghosts and spirits make frequent appearances in his books), and his seemingly encyclopedic knowledge of all kinds of interesting minutiae. While enjoying his intricate plots, you're also likely to learn a lot about such subjects as art forgery, opera, filmmaking, spiritualism and psychoanalysis. Davies's work deserves to be explored in depth, but a good place to start is with the three books comprising the Cornish trilogy, of which *What's Bred in the Bone* is the middle one (and my favorite).

DON DeLILLO
White Noise

White Noise offers a good example of DeLillo's capacity for being eerie, funny and touching all at the same time. This apocalyptic novel, about a professor of Hitler studies at a liberal arts college in middle America, explores what happens when an accident releases a lethal cloud of toxic chemicals into the air and causes him to face the possibility of his impending death. Highly entertaining, it is also an effective critique of our culture and its attitudes toward the big questions. Also worth reading is his much-acclaimed *Underworld.*

PETER DeVRIES
The Mackerel Plaza

DeVries's delightful skewering of liberal theology and middle-class life is extremely funny. DeVries lost his faith while a student at Calvin College, but remnants of his former worldview remain to deeply influence his work. This book is perhaps the high-water mark for a talented but overlooked comic genius.

E. L. DOCTOROW
Ragtime
City of God

Ragtime, with its accurate and entertaining portrait of an earlier time in American life, is probably Doctorow's best-known work. The more recent *City of God* is a clever intellectual stew of converging stories (a maverick priest, an ultra-modern rabbi, a Holocaust survivor, a *New York Times* reporter and so on) and literary devices (the notebook of a novelist, commentaries on popular songs, taped interviews, sketches for story and film ideas) that explore the intersection of the sacred and the profane in modern times. Difficult to follow at times but rewarding in its variety of insights.

DAVID JAMES DUNCAN
The River Why
The Brothers K

Duncan is a writer of abundant gifts. Though his novels deal with serious issues, they are filled with riotous humor. *The Brothers K* was one of the most enjoyable and moving reading experiences I have had in recent years. This tragic, funny, profound look at a family whose life is built around baseball is full of insight into the decade of the 1960s and how it helped to create the cultural environment in which we live. Christian readers will find some hysterical and moving moments centering on the faith of several of the main characters.

> Again his question hit me where I lived: I pictured rivers—December rivers, mist-shrouded and cold—and thigh deep in the long glides stood fishermen who'd arisen before dawn. . . . There they stood in the first gray light, in rain, wind, snowfall or frost; silent, patient, casting and casting again, retrieving nothing yet never questioning the possibility of bright steelhead hidden beneath the green slicks; numb-fingered, empty-bellied, aching-backed they stood . . . grumbling but vigilant, willing to pay hard penance for the mere chance of a sudden, subtle strike. What was a fisherman but an untransmuted seeker? And how much longer must be the wait, how much greater the skill, how much more infinite the patience and intense the vigilance in the search for the gift men called *the soul?*
>
> DAVID JAMES DUNCAN, *The River Why*

UMBERTO ECO
The Name of the Rose

This international bestseller is both a detailed evocation of monastic life in the fourteenth century and a penetrating mystery story. When monks start turning up murdered, Brother William turns detective to solve the mystery, armed with the logic of Aristotle, the theology of Aquinas and the empirical insights of Roger Bacon. Along the way to solving the crime, we are treated to an examination of church life, dogma, heresy and the nature of faith, as well as a meditation on the importance of books. A modern classic.

CLYDE EDGERTON
Raney
Walking Across Egypt
Killer Diller

Clyde Edgerton is one of the most amusing writers on the scene today, especially when he is dealing with religion Southern style. *Raney* deals with the marital struggles faced by a mismatched newlywed couple (she is a Southern Baptist, he a Yankee and Episcopalian). *Walking Across Egypt* (a meditation on the biblical injunction of lending aid to "the least of these") and *Killer Diller* share the same characters and are, at the same time, warmhearted and very funny. One of Edgerton's many delights is his marvelous ability with dialogue and regional accents.

RALPH ELLISON
Invisible Man

A gripping and satisfying novel about a young black man's search for identity in a society where his color makes him virtually invisible. Extremely well written, with biting social realism standing toe-to-toe with passages of surrealistic and heavily symbolic experimental writing. Many, including me, consider it among the very best of modern novels.

SHUSAKU ENDO
The Silence

Writing as a Christian in a Japan, a culture where Christians are a very small minority, Endo has received wide acclaim from Christians and non-Christians alike for his gripping tales about the struggle of faith in an unbelieving world. *The Silence* is a harrowing tale about the persecution of Christians in old Japan. Without romanticizing he shows the heroism of true commitment in the laying down of our lives (and our reputations) for our brothers and sisters.

LOUISE ERDRICH
Love Medicine

This gripping multigenerational story of two Native American families explores the anger, desire and healing power of love that make up their lives.

Erdrich is a writer who can be simultaneously lyrical and down-to-earth as she squarely faces the unique struggles of Native Americans. The story begun here continues in *The Beet Queen*, *Tracks* and *The Bingo Palace*.

PENELOPE FITZGERALD
The Blue Flower

Fitzgerald's economical writing style works effectively in this award-winning short novel based on the life of a German Romantic poet, Novalis. In this novel, as in other Fitzgerald books, the focus is more on the details of daily living than on the construction of an elaborate plot. Some will find this delightful, others potentially frustrating.

CHARLES FRAZIER
Cold Mountain

A lyrical, and at times harrowing, story about a soldier during the Civil War who tries to leave the battle behind to return to Ada, his prewar sweetheart. The trials he faces on his long journey homeward are almost unbearably grim, but the force of love is the power that impels him forward. A vivid and memorable work.

JOSTEIN GAARDER
Sophie's World

Subtitled *A Novel About the History of Philosophy*, this is a playful Norwegian novel that introduces the reader to the thinking and beliefs that have shaped our culture. As you are impelled along by an increasingly puzzling mystery, Gaarder offers a painless course in philosophy. Even when the story occasionally becomes swamped by its intention to teach us, we can forgive Mr. Gaarder, for we know we are in the hands of a marvelous instructor. Also worth investigating is the less philosophical *The Solitaire Mystery*.

ERNEST GAINES
A Lesson Before Dying

So convincing that it feels more like memoir than novel, *A Lesson Before Dying* is the deeply moral story of a young man awaiting execution for his part in a bungled robbery-murder and the school teacher who, unwillingly at first, reaches out to teach him to read, to write and to learn what it means to be a human being. In the manner in which it deals with prejudice, this is the kind of book that shows how morally powerful and dignified fiction can be.

GABRIEL GARCÍA MÁRQUEZ
One Hundred Years of Solitude
Love in a Time of Cholera

One Hundred Years of Solitude is a classic novel from South America that falls into the category of magic realism, an artful mix of fantasy and reality. In it events that are odd or supernatural are treated with as much seriousness as the moments of realism. And some of García Márquez's sensuous descriptive passages are pure poetry. Don't miss this long, multigenerational love story. Many of its scenes will impress themselves unforgettably into the reader's memory. *Love in a Time of Cholera* is another wondrously strange novel, recounting a moving story of unrequited love and a hope that never gives up.

> Then they went into Jose Arcadio Buendia's room, shook him as hard as they could, shouted in his ear, put a mirror in front of his nostrils, but they could not awaken him. A short time later, when the carpenter was taking measurements for the coffin, through the window they saw a light rain of tiny yellow flowers falling. They fell on the town all through the night in a silent storm, and they covered roofs and blocked the doors and smothered the animals who slept outdoors. So many flowers fell from the sky that in the morning the streets were carpeted with a compact cushion and they had to clear them away with shovels and rakes so that the funeral procession could pass by.
> GABRIEL GARCÍA MÁRQUEZ, *One Hundred Years of Solitude*

DENISE GIARDINA
Saints and Villains

In her novelization of the life of German theologian Dietrich Bonhoeffer, Giardina has avoided the hazard of sentimentalizing her subject or making him into a plaster saint. Instead, she gives us an incredibly well-researched and delicately nuanced picture of one who was both a flawed human being and also a hero and martyr for the faith. Here is one of those cases where a true story is the highest drama.

GAIL GODWIN
Father Melancholy's Daughter
Evensong

With the graceful pace of a nineteenth-century novel, *Father Melancholy's Daughter* unfolds the moving story of a loving Episcopal priest who struggles with doubt and depression, the wife who leaves him and his relationship with his almost-grown daughter. Its themes of family, faith and forgiveness are brought forward with artful storytelling. In fact, Godwin has dealt with issues of faith in a way that puts many more self-consciously Christian novels to shame. It is quite simply one of the best religious novels of recent years. *Evensong*, the sequel, is a somewhat lesser achievement but still a worthwhile read.

WILLIAM GOLDING
The Lord of the Flies
The Spire

The Lord of the Flies is the disturbing tale of a group of young boys who land on a deserted island and proceed to descend into brutal violence and murder. It is a telling illustration of the corrupt nature of humanity and of the violence that lies just beneath the surface of human civilization. *The Spire*, a parabolic story about a priest fixated on the idea of building a towering spire "to the glory of God," exposes the egotism that often coexists with religious enthusiasm.

JOHN GRISHAM
The Testament

Grisham made his name with pot-boiling legal thrillers, high on the readability quotient if undistinguished in the quality of their writing. In *The Testament* Grisham (who is a committed Baptist) has fashioned another such story, this time with a clearly evangelical message. A cynical lawyer travels into the depths of the jungle to let a young missionary woman know that she has become the heir to an enormous fortune. Some of the dialogue between the two is as forthright as a reading of Campus Crusade's four spiritual laws. Although one might wish for more subtlety and artfulness at points, it is nonetheless encouraging to see the gospel explained so clearly in a manner that has reached millions of readers. And in the process, Grisham has created a real page-turner, filled with unexpected pleasures, twists and turns.

PHILIP GULLEY
Home to Harmony

This charming and funny collection of short stories by a Quaker minister center on the adventures of a new pastor in a mythical small town called Harmony, a "tiny town hidden beneath the staple in the Rand McNally *Atlas.*" Filled with quaint characters and down-home wisdom, Gulley has created a wonderful little world that you'll be glad you visited.

> When I was in the second grade, my teacher, Miss Maxwell, read from *The Harmony Herald* that one in four children lived in China. I remember looking over the room, guessing which children they might be. I wasn't sure where China was, but suspected it was on bus route three. I recall being grateful I didn't live in China because I didn't care for Chinese food and couldn't speak the language.
> PHILIP GULLEY, *Home to Harmony*

DAVID GUTERSON
Snow Falling on Cedars

Densely atmospheric, this award-winning mystery is the story of the murder of a local fisherman on one of the islands in the Puget Sound in the 1950s. A beautiful meditation on desire and forgiveness, it also has a heart-wrenching love story and a thrilling courtroom drama. The story builds gradually and steadily, just like the snow on the Pacific Northwest cedars, until it reaches its moment of truth. A gorgeous piece of writing.

HELENE HANFF
84, Charing Cross Road

This slim volume is a joy for everyone who loves books. It is a breezy, funny and touching collection of the transatlantic letters (spanning twenty years) between a sassy New York writer, Helene Hanff, and the owner of a small British bookshop that specializes in rare books. Intermingled with requests for various books are Hanff's observations on life, literature, the war (much of the book takes place during World War II) and the budding love that grows between these two unlikely companions. Utterly charming!

RON HANSEN
Mariette in Ecstasy
Atticus

What happens when an attractive seventeen-year-old girl enters a convent in upstate New York and begins to experience, just as Christ once did, bleeding from her hands, feet and side? Hansen's vivid and restrained novel shows the turmoil these manifestations cause and the questions they raise about her sanity, integrity and relationship with God. Behind the quiet and commonplace, Hansen seems to be suggesting, lies a world of mystery and transcendence. Beautifully crafted, as are other Hansen novels, including his modern version of the prodigal son story, *Atticus*.

JON HASSLER
Staggerford
Simon's Night

It was difficult to decide which of Hassler's many wonderful novels to suggest, so I took the easy way out, choosing his first two major works. *Staggerford* centers on a thirty-five-year-old bachelor high school literature teacher and the events that cause uproar in his peaceful and predictable world. *Simon's Night* tells the story of what happens to a retired university professor who, fearing the onset of decrepitude, voluntarily commits himself to a home for the elderly. As with all of Hassler's books, these two are gentle and warm-hearted yet, at the same time, unsparingly realistic about the struggles of being human. There is also a streak of faith that runs through many of Hassler's novels, mirroring his own religious commitment. If you enjoy these two, try *The Love Hunter, A Green Journey, Dear James, Rookery Blues* and *North of Hope*.

JOSEPH HELLER
Catch-22

One of the funniest books ever written, *Catch-22* is a darkly comic modern classic about the foolishness of war and the weakness of human nature. Set in World War II, Heller's book tells the story about a bomber pilot who no longer wants to fly his bombing mission. However, he must deal with absurd military regulations, career-centered military men, greedy opportunists and a host of other unforgettable characters. The *New York Times* described the novel as "wildly original, brutally gruesome, a dazzling performance, vulgarly, bitterly, savagely funny, unforgettable." That it certainly is.

MARK HELPRIN
A Soldier of the Great War
Memoir from Antproof Case

Gorgeous descriptive writing, breathtaking flights of fantasy, memorable characters, quirky humor, and labyrinthine plots: these are the elements that blend into the wondrous concoction that is a Mark Helprin novel. He creates a reading experience that is uniquely his own and adds a touch of seriousness by his concern for moral and spiritual issues. Rarely has a novel affected me as deeply as did Helprin's *A Soldier of the Great War*. A grand, sweeping epic, it mixes realism with playful embellishment as it meditates on such issues as beauty, love, passion and the meaning of life. If you enjoy these two novels, you'll want to explore his collections of short stories (especially *Ellis Island*) and other novels, such as *A Winter's Tale* and *Refiner's Fire*.

> I asked myself, why do I love, and what is the power of beauty, and I understood that each and every instance of beauty is a promise and example, in miniature, of life that can end in balance, with symmetry, purpose, and hope—even if without explanation. Beauty has no explanation, but its right perfection elicits love. I wondered if my life would be the same, if at the end the elements would come together just enough to give rise to a simple melody as powerful as the one in Paolo's metal top, a song that, even if it did not explain the desperate and painful past, would make it worthy of love.
>
> Of course, I still don't know. God help me to have a moment of his saddest beauty in which I do. MARK HELPRIN, *A Soldier of the Great War*

OSCAR HIJUELOS
Mr. Ives' Christmas

In this novel, the Pulitzer Prize-winning novelist traces the life story of Mr. Ives, a devoutly religious man. Ives lives a happy and fulfilled life until the day his seventeen-year-old son, to whom he is deeply devoted, is gunned down by a teenage thug. This tragedy occurs during the Christmas season, just months before the son is to enter seminary. Suddenly Ives finds himself questioning everything, wrestling with doubt and deep despair as he tries to rebuild the shattered foundations of his life and belief. Tender and beautifully written, this novel traces the journey of a man striving to hold onto his faith in a violent and increasingly faithless world.

SUSAN HOWATCH
Glittering Images
Glamorous Powers

Howatch's series of novels about the clergy in the fictional English village of Starbridge are not without their faults: the plot and dialogue sometimes become a bit overwrought, and some of the psychologizing is excessive. These faults aside, however, Howatch has managed to accomplish something significant and important in these novels. She has produced a realistic and engrossing glimpse into the struggle of faith in our modern world. Her characters are not saints in the medieval sense of the word. They struggle against the temptations of the flesh: power, status and especially sex. Along the way we gain rich insights into the importance of facing the reality of our own hidden sin if we are to exult in the miracle of grace and forgiveness. These are the type of books you could give to a nonbeliever to open up rich channels of discussion and witness. The series continues with *Ultimate Prizes, Scandalous Risks, Mystical Paths, Absolute Truths, The Wonder Worker* and *High Flyer.*

JOHN IRVING
A Prayer for Owen Meany

An often very funny episodic novel with a marvelous grasp of the providence of God. Owen Meany is a young misfit who comes to believe that he has been chosen to be an instrument of God. By the end of the novel, readers may think that he's right. Irving was once a student of Frederick Buechner, and the influence shows in the humorous and touching ways he deals with issues of faith, as well as in the childlike sense of wonder his characters show in the face of miracles. The stunning conclusion of the book places this novel in that small circle of contemporary novels that take the miraculous seriously.

JAN KARON
At Home in Mitford

This is the first in Karon's genial little series of books about a fictional North Carolina town and its inhabitants, especially the kind and faithful Episcopal rector, Father Tim. *Publisher's Weekly* described this book as a "cozy, neighborly read," and that captures pretty well the tone of the stories. Although originally released by a Christian publisher, these books proved so popular that they were picked up by a major general market publisher and have received wide distribution. While not the most deeply profound books you're likely to read this year, there is something infectiously modest and appealing about their warm-hearted authenticity. They demonstrate what it looks like to live out the Christian life on a day-to-day basis. The series continues with *A Light in the Window, These High Green Hills, Out to Canaan* and *A New Song*.

GARRISON KEILLOR
Lake Wobegon Days

This first novel by the host of the radio program *Prairie Home Companion* is a delightful and funny collection of stories related to his fictional Minnesota town, Lake Wobegon. The book is enjoyable throughout, but Christians may especially get a chuckle out of his stories of the religious infighting among the saints who dwell in the town. A good demonstration of why grace is so important in our relationships with one another.

STEPHEN KING
The Green Mile

King is best known for his bestselling horror stories, but here the outbreaking of the supernatural is more benign as he explores the events surrounding a gentle giant of a prisoner on death row who has healing powers. *The Green Mile* is a page-turner, complete with a twisting plot, memorable characters and sense of wonder. Originally produced as a serial novel (which is a fun way to read it), *The Green Mile* has now been rereleased in one volume.

BARBARA KINGSOLVER
The Poisonwood Bible
Animal Dreams

One can't fault Barbara Kingsolver for not being passionate enough about her politics. One *can* criticize the occasional political heavy-handedness. Each of her books has a point she wants to drive home, which can sometimes conflict with her storytelling. Still, it is refreshing to read an author who cares so deeply and is willing to take a stand. *The Poisonwood Bible* is her flawed masterpiece, an epic novel written from a variety of perspectives about an American missionary to the Congo, whose family pays dearly for his stubborn (and often ill-considered) devotion. While not a flattering picture of missions (and not entirely fair), it does grapple with some of the problems related to bringing the gospel to another culture. But the strength of her characters and the way she has given them each such a distinctive voice make this book unforgettable.

> "Tata Jesus is bangala!" declares the Reverend every Sunday at the end of his sermon. More and more, mistrusting his interpreters, he tries to speak in Kikongo. He throws back his head and shouts these words to the sky, while his lambs sit scratching themselves in wonder. *Bangala* means something precious and dear. But the way he pronounces it, it means the poisonwood tree. Praise the Lord, hallelujah, my friends! For Jesus will make you itch like nobody's business.
> BARBARA KINGSOLVER, *The Poisonwood Bible*

HARPER LEE
To Kill a Mockingbird

Harper Lee tells the story of a white Southern lawyer who fights enormous odds in defending a young black man accused of rape. This powerful novel about the power of conscience is charged with a quiet heroism. Seen through the eyes of the lawyer's two young children, *To Kill a Mockingbird* unearths the hypocrisy and prejudice of racism as it operates in a small Southern town.

MADELEINE L'ENGLE
A Wrinkle in Time
A Ring of Endless Light

The Time Tetralogy, which begins with the award-winning *A Wrinkle in Time*, subtly explores theological issues in the guise of science fiction. While not as straightforward as the Chronicles of Narnia (and perhaps not as strictly orthodox either), these and other books by L'Engle give evidence of an alive and vibrant faith and a very personal vision. Readers will enjoy her memorable characters, vivid descriptions and celebration of family life. The titles in the series include *A Wrinkle in Time*, *A Wind in the Door*, *A Swiftly Tilting Planet* and *Many Waters*. *Ring of Endless Light* is from another fine series of novels (also intended for young adults, but enjoyable for anyone who likes good books) based on the Austin family.

BERNARD MALAMUD
The Assistant
The Fixer

These are two of the finest novels by one of the greatest Jewish writers of our time. *The Assistant* tells the moving story of a young man who robs a Jewish merchant and then returns to work in his shop in an attempt at redeeming himself. *The Fixer* is a more epic work and deals with the plight of Russian Jews.

DON MILLER
Prayer and the Art of Volkswagen Maintenance

This is the playful first work of a young writer of great promise. Miller's genre here is embellished autobiography as he tells the mostly true story of a cross-country road trip in an undependable Volkswagen bus, searching for adventure and for a more authentic faith. This is *On the Road* with a distinctly Christian slant. The dialogue between Miller and his traveling partner is priceless, and their adventures both funny and faith-building. Along the way, the two young men argue and debate the weaknesses of "church culture" and look for new ways to deepen and express their Christian commitment. Miller's is a fresh voice for a new generation of young believers.

WALTER MILLER
A Canticle for Leibowitz

Centuries after the earth has been nearly destroyed by a "flame deluge" (a nuclear war), the monks of the Order of St. Leibowitz struggle to preserve ancient knowledge in a new dark age. They preserve the precious relics of their founder, St. Leibowitz (including the sacred shrine of "Fallout Shelter"), in their Utah monastery, and they witness humanity's rebirth from the ashes. A mixture of science fiction, cultural critique and religious reflection, *A Canticle for Leibowitz* contains much food for thought about the struggle of faith and reason.

TONI MORRISON
Beloved

Morrison won the Pulitzer Prize for this shattering novel about an escaped slave who is haunted by her past. With this novel, Morrison established herself as one of the premier writers in modern American literature. This distinguished and poetic indictment of slavery works at every level, leaving readers feeling as though they have passed through the fire with Sethe, the proud and heartbroken heroine.

MICHAEL D. O'BRIEN
Father Elijah

This apocalyptic novel is about a Jewish convert, a Holocaust survivor who becomes a Carmelite priest and is called out of twenty years of obscurity in a Middle Eastern monastery to assist the pope by penetrating into the inner circle of the man the Vatican has come to believe may be the antichrist. If you can imagine what it might have been like if Dostoyevsky had attempted to write a thriller, you'll have some idea of the many levels on which this novel works. Widely hailed by serious critics on its release, O'Brien has penned a novel that is literate, satirical, spiritually profound and thoroughly entertaining.

ALAN PATON
Cry, the Beloved Country

Paton's classic novel about South Africa was an immediate worldwide best-seller and opened many eyes to the tragic state of apartheid. It is the moving story of a Zulu pastor who travels to the city to try to rescue his prodigal son, Absalom, who is charged with the murder of a promising young white man who was working for equal rights for black Africans. A powerful tale of redemption and forgiveness, Paton's novel demonstrates the ability of fiction to expand our hearts and make us think in a more Christlike manner.

WALKER PERCY
The Moviegoer
Love in the Ruins
The Second Coming
Lost in the Cosmos: The Last Self-Help Book

Quite possibly my favorite modern novelist, Walker Percy brings to his work a unique blend of scientific precision in his powers of observation, a deep commitment to the Christian worldview, quirky Southern humor and a vast intellect. Percy's books focus on the existential quandaries of the modern person and lay bare the aimlessness and ennui of our culture. As a cultural critic he is unparalleled, but that never gets in the way of his creating a wonderful reading experience. And he is very funny! I would suggest *The Second Coming* (which has nothing to do with eschatology) as the best place to start exploring his work. Be forewarned that Percy is a thoroughly modern novelist and deals with issues of life in an unflinching and honest way. His frankness adds much to the overriding message of his work: human beings cannot survive with sanity and truth unless God is granted his rightful place in their lives.

Lost in the Cosmos is a nonfiction work; a strange, hilarious, profound meditation on the human condition, the kind of book Kierkegaard might have written had he lived at the end of the twentieth century. To learn more about the life and thought of this brilliant writer, I'd recommend the excellent biography *Pilgrim in the Ruins* by Jay Toulson.

> I, for example, am a Roman Catholic, albeit a bad one. I believe in the Holy Catholic Apostolic and Roman Church, in God the Father, in the election of the Jews, in Jesus Christ His Son our Lord, who founded the Church on Peter his first vicar, which will last until the end of the world. Some years ago, however, I stopped eating Christ in Communion, stopped going to mass, and have since fallen into a disorderly life. I believe in God and the whole business but I love women best, music and science next, whiskey next, God fourth, and my fellowman hardly at all. Generally I do as I please. A man, wrote John, who says he believes in God and does not keep his commandments is a liar. If John is right, then I am a liar. Nevertheless, I still believe. WALKER PERCY, *Love in the Ruins*

ROBERT PIRSIG
Zen and the Art of Motorcycle Maintenance

Pirsig's philosophical novel about a man's journey in search of himself and the meaning of his life asks all the right questions and points toward meanings that transcend our material existence. In the pages of the novel, he approaches the question of life's meaning as a mechanic would approach the repair of a motorcycle, taking us step by step through all the stages as he pursues the truth about himself and about what is really important in life. Though most Christians will find Pirsig's answers to be inadequate, his journey toward truth makes very worthwhile reading.

CHAIM POTOK
The Chosen
The Promise
My Name Is Asher Lev

Most of Potok's books are about young Jewish protagonists in search of how they can relate their Jewish heritage to the modern world. Evangelicals will no doubt identify with the struggles that Potok's young men and women face in holding fast to a traditional faith in a cosmopolitan and secular world. *The Chosen* is typical of Potok's novels: gentle, full of love and compassion yet honest in its depiction of struggle. Its sequel, *The Promise,* is nearly as good as its worthy predecessor. *My Name Is Asher Lev* is a more melancholy tale, the story of a young artistic prodigy whose family is part of a very strict Jewish community and sees little value (and much danger) in his artistic pursuit. Asher Lev attempts to find a way to exercise his God-given talent while, at the same time, valuing the heritage of his family.

THOMAS PYNCHON
Gravity's Rainbow

A demanding, bizarre, experimental but ultimately powerful antiwar novel by a reclusive genius. It tells the story of an American lieutenant stationed in London during World War II who has an unusual gift: his erections anticipate German rocket launches. Vulgar yet extraordinary, it is considered by many critics to be among the very best and most original novels of our time. If the book seems daunting in its length, try *The Crying of Lot 49,* a much shorter novel.

ARUNDHATI ROY
The God of Small Things

Quite possibly the most beautifully written novel I have read in quite some time, *The God of Small Things*, a novel about life and love and passion in India, is full of sensuous and evocative prose. People seem to have two differing responses to this book. Either they find it overwritten and too hard to follow, or they luxuriate in the densely poetic prose, delighting in the vivid descriptiveness. I'm in the latter category; in fact, I consider the book a near masterpiece.

> "D'you know what happens when you hurt people?" Ammu said. "When you hurt people, they begin to love you less. That's what careless words do. They make people love you a little less."
>
> A cold moth with unusually dense dorsal tufts landed lightly on Rahel's heart. Where its icy legs touched her, she got goosebumps. Six goosebumps on her careless heart.
>
> A little less her Ammu loved her.
>
> And so, out the gate, up the road, and to the left. The taxi stand. A hurt mother, an ex-nun, a hot child and a cold one. Six goosebumps and a moth . . . The moth on Rahel's heart spread its velvet wings, and the chill crept into her bones. ARUNDHATI ROY, *The God of Small Things*

MARY DORIA RUSSELL
The Sparrow

An interesting futuristic science fiction tale with profound moral implications, *The Sparrow* relates what happens when a group of people, including scientists and priests, travels across the galaxy to the planet Rakhat. This group of agnostics and true believers encounters a world they had not expected to find and must deal with the disastrous results of their mission. Startling and inventive, the story begun here is continued in *The Children of God*.

J. D. SALINGER
The Catcher in the Rye
Franny and Zooey

The Catcher in the Rye is an infamous book about a young man stifled by meaningless conformity and the shallowness of the values of those adults around him. Salinger accurately captures an adolescent frame of mind. The rough language (which has caused the book to be censored by numerous schools) adds to the portrait of an unhappy young man on a quest for authenticity in a world of phonies. A fascinating book, *Franny and Zooey* is somewhat more mannered in its style; its themes should prove of great interest to Christian readers.

FRANK SCHAEFFER
Portofino
Saving Grandma

Who would have thought that the son of famous philosopher/evangelist Francis Schaeffer would one day use his family's European missionary experiences as fodder for such a witty and sarcastic look at the foibles of fundamentalism? The books are sometimes funny, occasionally a bit unsettling but always insightful; those who grew up in the evangelical or fundamentalist culture will recognize themselves and their upbringing in these delightful novels. If you are able to laugh at yourself, you are sure to enjoy *Portofino* and its sequel, *Saving Grandma*.

ISAAC BASHEVIS SINGER
Gimpel the Fool
The Penitent

Singer is a Yiddish writer who delightfully captures the warmth and mystery of Jewish life through the ages. In his books humor and the supernatural are wedded to create a unique reading experience. His best work is probably found in his short story collections (of which *Gimpel the Fool* is an example), but readers will find treasures amidst all his work. *The Penitent* is a powerful tale of a convert to orthodox Judaism.

ALEXANDER SOLZHENITSYN
One Day in the Life of Ivan Denisovich
The First Circle
Cancer Ward
The Gulag Archipelago
Nobel Lecture

Solzhenitsyn's own life is a paradigm of moral courage. He follows in the great Russian tradition of Tolstoy and Dostoyevsky in using his writing to explore humanity in the most extreme of situations. His brilliant novels explore the twin capacity of human beings for both unspeakable cruelty and unbelievable courage. Usually, it is faith in God that gives his characters the ability to carry on in the worst of circumstances. As a writer and as a person, Solzhenitsyn stands in an exalted position among modern writers. *One Day in the Life* will serve as a good introduction to Solzhenitsyn's work. However, I prefer his longer novels, such as *The First Circle* and *Cancer Ward*, which give him more room to do what he does best: create a completely believable world, peopled with a variety of conflicting worldviews, all struggling to find a moral foundation by which to live.

> If only there were evil people somewhere insidiously committing evil deeds and it were necessary only to separate them from the rest of us and destroy them. But the line dividing good and evil cuts through the heart of every human being. And who is willing to destroy a piece of his own heart?
> ALEXANDER SOLZHENITSYN, *The Gulag Archipelago*

JOHN KENNEDY TOOLE
A Confederacy of Dunces

Ignatius J. Reilly is a slovenly, self-proclaimed genius living in New Orleans who is in revolt against the entire twentieth century. In this hilarious and farcical book, Toole employs biting satire and savage wit to tell his story about a modern Don Quixote, doing battle with all he finds disagreeable in the modern world. Toole's own story is tragic. He committed suicide at age thirty-two, an unpublished author whose manuscript had been rejected by numerous publishers. His mother, persistently confident in her son's talent, was able to convince Walker Percy to take a look at this manuscript. Percy knew it was a work of comic genius and put it in the right hands. It was published to great critical acclaim, but too late for its author to enjoy the applause.

ANNE TYLER
Saint Maybe
The Accidental Tourist
The Patchwork Planet

No author I know of seems to be so genuinely compassionate toward her characters as Anne Tyler. Because she seems to care so much, the reader comes to feel the same sort of deep sympathy. She often builds her stories around the inner dynamics of families and the mysteries that hold them together. Her prose style is straightforward and graceful, warmed by her humor and her attention to the little details of life. *Saint Maybe* is a good place to begin. It's the story of Ian Bedloe, who blames himself for the accidental death of his older brother. Broken by depression and a crippling secret guilt, Ian discovers a sign reading "Church of the Second Chance"; there he discovers the road to forgiveness through sacrifice and love. *Saint Maybe* is beautiful, touching and wholly convincing. Nearly all Tyler's novels are worth exploring.

SIGRID UNDSET
Kristin Lavransdatter

The Norwegian novelist Sigrid Undset was a Nobel Prize winner, and this is her masterpiece. A grand historical epic set in fourteenth century Norway, *Kristin Lavransdatter* tells the story of a passionate and strong-willed woman who chooses love over duty and familial approval. Few writers have so convincingly captured the world of the Middle Ages. Unset deals with issues of love, faith and passion in such a way that some critics have compared her to Dostoyevsky. Kristin's story is contained in three volumes: *The Bridal Wreath, The Mistress of Husaby* and *The Cross*.

JOHN UPDIKE
Rabbit, Run
Roger's Version
In the Beauty of the Lilies

Updike is a fine novelist with a stunningly beautiful prose style. Many of his novels have theological themes, especially *Rabbit, Run* and the following three: *A Month of Sundays* tells the story of a minister struggling with his libido (and contains some marvelous sermons); *Roger's Version* deals with a young computer wiz who is convinced he has found scientific proof of God's existence; and *In the Beauty of the Lilies* covers several generations in a family that wavers between faith and doubt. Each demonstrates a keen theological awareness. However, some may find his fixation on sexual issues to be a little too graphic and anatomically detailed for their taste. Nonetheless, he writes with a graceful style and has a sensitive ability to take us inside the minds and emotions of his characters. His autobiographical *Self-Consciousness* is a personal look at his interests and obsessions, including his religious ones.

ELIZABETH DEWBERRY VAUGHN
Many Things Have Happened Since He Died

This stunning first novel shows great promise for Ms. Vaughn, who writes in the voice of a poorly educated Southern girl who is fiercely passionate and hopelessly naive. This narrator speaks of her devotion to the religion of her childhood and of the pain of her life with an abusive husband. Funny, heart-wrenching and enchanting, Vaughn's book has captured an authentic voice that is unforgettable in its strength in the midst of tragedy. A great and gutsy book.

KURT VONNEGUT
Cat's Cradle
Slaughterhouse Five

The crazed and absurd universe of Kurt Vonnegut is revealed best in these two satirical novels. Vonnegut's kindhearted nihilism is compelling to many readers who cannot make sense of the violent and heartless tendencies of modern civilization. This has made him something of a guru to many—a role he studiously shuns. If, like me, you find these two novels to be uproariously funny, amazingly inventive and utterly fascinating, you'll also want to explore some of his other books, especially *Player Piano* and *Bluebeard*.

SUSAN VREELAND
Girl in Hyacinth Blue

Vreeland's lyrical collection of connected short stories follows the progress of an unrecognized painting by the Dutch master Vermeer down through several generations. A tender examination of the irreplaceable role that art plays in our lives and a pointer toward the beauty waiting to be found in the very ordinary things that surround us.

ALICE WALKER
The Color Purple

This novel unfolds in an impoverished and abused black woman's letters to God and to her sister; it underscores the oppression of black women in their relationships with whites and with black men. Celie's story is a testament to the power of women's friendships and to the ability to survive and maintain dignity in the face of injustice, oppression and betrayal. Written with simplicity, grace and a gritty realism.

WALTER WANGERIN
The Book of the Dun Cow
Ragman and Other Cries of Faith
The Book of God

An ordained Lutheran minister, Wangerin once served an inner-city black congregation where he and his family were the only white members. He also taught at a seminary before dedicating himself to write full time. Wangerin's ability to craft one beautiful sentence after another and to deeply move the reader without becoming mawkish or sentimental make his books a rare and highly enjoyable reading experience. *The Book of the Dun Cow* is an award-winning fantasy that takes place in a barnyard. Its somber sequel, *The Book of Sorrows*, is equally powerful. *Ragman and Other Cries of Faith* is a collection of short stories, poems and meditations that perhaps showcase Wangerin's talent at its best. One of his most recent works, *The Book of God*, is a dramatic and convincing retelling of the whole biblical story, filled with insight and emotion.

> A door had opened in the universe, and through my son, and in my face. The glory of the Lord had burst from a little child. Not Sunday School lessons, nor all the sermons he had heard me preach, nor the smattering of the Bible reading that the child had done, but Jesus Christ himself was the cause of the most dramatic and real wonder. Matthew didn't speak the Christ; for an instant Matthew *was* the Christ—or rather, was Christ abode in him, and I saw it; not with my eyes, for that was his own short-fingered hand on my knee, but with my soul, to which the Word had penetrated, changing it. He had done so casually what in fact he could not do. Only God could do that. But it was most certainly done: I was forgiven indeed. WALTER WANGERIN, *Ragman and Other Cries of Faith*

PENELOPE WILCOCK
The Hawk and the Dove
The Wounds of God
The Long Fall

In these wonderful Christian novels, Wilcock reaches back through the centuries to an ancient monastery and shows God's grace at work in the daily round of lives of the monks. In each of the three installments we see these men break through to a more honest evaluation of themselves and of their need for God and for each other. Her stories are simple on the surface, but are actually honest and deeply felt investigations of the human heart. Each book resonates with a clear understanding of the love and mercy of God.

VINITA HAMPTON WRIGHT
Grace at Bender Springs

Many novels published by Christian publishing companies suffer from a Pollyanna view of reality, filled with unconvincing conversions and lacking the gritty realities of human life. Wright's books are wonderful exceptions to this rule, and one hopes her success will help raise the level of this genre of writing above its usual propagandistic limitations. In *Grace at Bender Springs* Wright tells several interlocking stories, including those of a pastor's wife who is struggling to keep her faith and her sanity, and a young man who is toying with the idea of committing suicide. The dialogue and motivations of her characters are honest and believable. Because of this honesty, when Wright delivers spiritual insights, they are usually convincing and convicting. She is a good model for the right way to create a religious novel. *Velma Still Cooks at Leeway* is a worthy follow-up novel, also based in her fictional town of Bender Springs.

NINE

GREAT BOOKS FOR YOUNG READERS

*No book is really worth reading at the age of ten
which is not equally (and often far more)
worth reading at the age of fifty and beyond.*
C. S. LEWIS

One of the greatest gifts we can give to our children is to introduce them to the joys of reading. In a culture whose primary source of entertainment is television, books may seem to our children to involve a lot more effort than sitting in front of the television set. But books are also so much more satisfying than the bulk of what is available on TV. As mothers and fathers, grandparents and teachers, we can help our kids discover the rewards that reading offers, how fun and exciting reading a good book can be.

But where do we start? I'd like to offer this list as a jumping-off place for beginning to explore children's literature. I've also tried (imperfectly, I'm certain) to suggest age-appropriate reading levels. Of course, you don't have to wait until your kids can read for them to begin to love books and reading. From the earliest ages, children love to be read to. Books they cannot read for themselves may be thoroughly enjoyed when you read aloud to them. And this enjoyment may continue longer than you'd think. Even my teenage daughters love it when Mom or Dad read aloud to the family!

Age Annotations

PS = preschoolers   GS = ages 6-10   YA = young adult   AA = all ages

---

Note: I feel a need to apologize for the imprecision of my recommendations in these age categories. What is appropriate for any one child will depend on his or her own level of maturity, reading skills and attention span. Every child is unique with respect to aptitude for reading and favorite kinds of books. These categorizations, then, serve only as a rough guide to the level of difficulty in comprehending each book. And, of course, children can comprehend some books they are unable to read themselves. Some seven-year-olds may be able to listen to and understand all but the most mature books on this list, while some children who are much older may be, at least initially, unable to sit still through even the shortest story.

AESOP
Fables

This ancient Greek classic is a collection of very short tales and proverbs that illustrate character strengths and flaws in action. It is a rich treasure of moral teaching for both young and old. Use a modern translation; due to their difficult language, some of the older ones obscure the meanings and messages in the stories. [AA]

LOUISA MAY ALCOTT
Little Women

This was my wife's favorite book as a child, and my two daughters have also appreciated its warm depiction of family life and its unflagging commitment to moral virtue. This book provides realistic yet powerful examples of morality for children and adults alike. [GS/YA]

HANS CHRISTIAN ANDERSEN
Andersen's Fairy Tales
BROTHERS GRIMM
Grimm's Fairy Tales

Two of the classic collections of fairy tales, these include most of the popular favorites. In their original versions they are more violent and less prone to happy endings than some of the modern versions of these tales. But they will make good fodder for family discussions of moral values and handling difficult situations. [PS/GS]

J. M. BARRIE
Peter Pan

A charming fantasy-adventure tale about a young boy who doesn't want to grow up. [GS/YA]

L. FRANK BAUM
The Wizard of Oz

Dorothy's adventures in Oz make for delightful and imagination-stirring reading. Along the way we are provided with a powerful picture of the human search to overcome personal inadequacies, and a realization that the resources for change are within everyone's grasp. [GS/YA]

MICHAEL BEDARD
Emily

Who is this unusual reclusive neighbor who writes poetry? This sweet little tale is about a girl who discovers that her neighbor is the famous poet Emily Dickinson. [GS]

LUDWIG BEMELMANS
Madeline

My daughters loved the rhymed story of Madeline, the little girl who is brave even when she faces having her appendix removed. [PS/GS]

WILLIAM J. BENNETT
The Book of Virtues

An indispensable collection of stories and extracts grouped together by the character qualities they teach. This hefty volume contains many hours' worth of valuable material for the whole family. By all means, buy it and use it. [AA]

JOHN BIBEE
The Magic Bicycle

This is the first in Bibee's Spirit Flyer series, a collection of stories about several children who discover extraordinary bicycles with magical abilities. They soon find themselves pitted against Goliath Toys, a toy manufacturer that wants the magical bikes destroyed. The writer's Christian commitment shines through the eight wonderful books in this series. Prepare for an exciting ride! [GS/YA]

CHRISTINA BJORK
Linnea in Monet's Garden

This charming story about a young girl who visits the garden of the great painter Monet affirms the importance of great art. [AA]

MICHAEL BOND
A Bear Called Paddington

The humorous misadventures of a lovable but none-too-bright bear, known for his oversized hat, blue duffle coat and red Wellington boots. [GS]

JAN BRETT
Beauty and the Beast

A good version of this classic tale, which teaches that beauty is more than skin-deep and that true love involves sacrifice. [GS/YA]

MARGARET WISE BROWN
Goodnight Moon
Runaway Bunny

Goodnight Moon is a very simple and soothing book to read to the very young before they go to bed. It seems to produce an environment of peacefulness for them. *Runaway Bunny* shows the persistent love of a mother bunny for her children. [PS]

JEAN DE BRUNHOFF
The Story of Babar

The story of a talking elephant's adventures in France and as king of the elephants. Delightful illustrations. [PS/GS]

JOHN BUNYAN
The Pilgrim's Progress

Children can best appreciate this classic Christian allegory of the spiritual life through an abridgment or adaptation. I especially recommend the adaptation entitled *Dangerous Journey*, which does a good job of putting the story within the reach of children without sacrificing its substance and power. [GS/YA]

FRANCES HODGSON BURNETT
The Secret Garden
The Little Princess

The Secret Garden is a magical tale about the transformation of an angry and selfish little girl through the healing power of love and friendship. *The Little Princess* teaches the virtues of compassion and consideration for others, even in the face of hardship. [GS/YA]

SHEILA BURNFORD
The Incredible Journey

An exciting tale about two dogs and a cat who brave the wilds in search of their owner. [YA]

NICK BUTTERWORTH AND MICK INKPEN
The Lost Sheep

This is the first of four delightful retellings of the parables. The illustrations and the text are both wonderful. [PS]

LEWIS CARROLL
Alice's Adventures in Wonderland
Alice Through the Looking Glass

The Alice stories are marked by a seemingly endless supply of wit and invention. They can be thoroughly enjoyed by all ages, but most children will enjoy them more when they are somewhat older. [AA]

SUSAN COOLIDGE
What Katy Did
A wonderfully moving story that follows the development of character and virtue in a young girl after a crippling accident. [GS/YA]

BARBARA COONEY
Miss Rumphius
Miss Rumphius wishes to leave her mark on the world and finds a beautiful way to do it. [GS]

ROALD DAHL
Charlie and the Chocolate Factory
A delightful, humorous tale about a young boy whose goodness and decency bring about the fulfillment of his dream. His fate is contrasted with those who are greedy, gluttonous, self-absorbed and disobedient. [GS/YA]

DANIEL DEFOE
Robinson Crusoe
This is the fascinating tale of a man stranded on a desert island who must learn to survive with his meager store of food and tools. Defoe's tale has explicit references to the sovereignty of God and our need to trust in him. The story raises many moral issues worth discussing. [YA]

TOMIE dePAOLA
The Clown of God
The very moving story of a beggar boy who becomes a famous juggler and learns to dedicate his gift to God. [AA]

CHARLES DICKENS
A Christmas Carol
The classic tale of a cruel and selfish man who discovers what is really important in life. *A Tale of Two Cities* is more difficult but also very rewarding. [YA/AA]

ARTHUR CONAN DOYLE
Sherlock Holmes stories

Beginning with *A Study in Scarlet*, Doyle wrote four novels and fifty-six short stories about his fictional detective. Holmes offers a marvelous model of how to use logical deductive thinking to solve problems. As a child I loved to curl up with one of these stories and lose myself in the foggy streets of Edwardian London. The books are exciting as well as intellectually challenging. The vocabulary is sometimes difficult, so they are recommended for older children. [YA]

CLIFTON FADIMAN
World Treasury of Children's Literature (two volumes)

Fadiman has gathered in these two volumes some of the finest writing for children of all time. The set includes poetry, short stories, myths and excerpts of longer stories. Both classic and modern pieces are included in this cornucopia of fine children's literature. This is a wonderful place to start building your collection of good books. [AA]

ANNE FRANK
The Diary of Anne Frank

The emotionally wrenching diary of a young girl whose family and friends suffered at the hands of Nazi Germany, this book teaches valuable lessons about tolerance, loyalty and the value of human life. [YA]

DON FREEMAN
Corduroy

An adorable bear finds the home he has always dreamed of. Absolutely sweet and delightful! [PS/GS]

KENNETH GRAHAME
The Wind in the Willows
The Reluctant Dragon

The Wind in the Willows is one of the most charming books ever written, with lovable characters and a deep sense of nostalgia for the innocence and wonder of childhood. Children enjoy its marvelous humor. *The Reluctant*

Dragon is a delightful story about a precocious boy and his friendship with a lazy and cowardly dragon. It provides a good model of how to explore difficult situations and find positive solutions. And its wry humor will make it a treat for adults as well. [AA]

FLORENCE PARRY HEIDE
The Shrinking of Treehorn
Treehorn's Treasure

Sophisticated and wryly humorous little tales about a boy who is always ignored and the bizarre, unexpected things that happen to him. [GS/AA]

JAMES HERRIOT
All Creatures Great and Small

The first in a series of delightful books about a young English veterinarian in the Yorkshire countryside. [YA/AA]

RUSSELL HOBAN
Bedtime for Frances
A Baby Sister for Frances
Bread and Jam for Frances

Wonderful books about a small, rather precocious badger. Children seem to find in Frances a mirror of their own fears, distastes and faults. *Bread and Jam for Frances* is a good cautionary tale for children who are picky eaters. [PS/GS]

ANGELA ELWELL HUNT
The Tale of Three Trees

Three trees each have a dream. One tree wants to become a treasure chest, one a ship and the third a sign for all mankind. Each of these dreams is fulfilled in unexpected ways by the power of God. A rich allegorical folktale about what God has done for us. [AA]

HANNAH HURNARD
Hind's Feet on High Places

This is an allegorical tale about the Christian life, seen through the eyes of

Much-Afraid as she searches for God's "high places." Valuable for helping young people realize that the life of faith sometimes requires struggle and sacrifice. [YA]

CROCKETT JOHNSON
Harold and the Purple Crayon
Armed with his purple crayon, Harold creates a whole world for himself and uses his imagination to get himself out of a number of potential dangers. [PS/GS]

RUDYARD KIPLING
The Jungle Book
Just So Stories
Kipling's much-loved animal tales teach us a lot about humans and the way we treat each other. Many good moral lessons and much humorous entertainment await the reader of his stories. [GS/YA]

CHARLES AND MARY LAMB
Tales from Shakespeare
The Lambs manage to capture much of the power and beauty of Shakespeare's dramas in their prose renditions. While no substitute for the bard himself, they are an excellent introduction to the riches your children can find later in reading the original plays for themselves. [GS/YA]

ANDREW LANG
The Blue Fairy Book
The Red Fairy Book
Lang has compiled a series of fairy-tale collections with each book named after a color. These are the real thing: unexpurgated originals. Be forewarned that the stories do not always have a happy ending and are often a bit grisly. [GS/YA]

MUNRO LEAF
The Story of Ferdinand
Gentle Ferdinand is a peaceful bull who would rather sit and smell the flow-

ers than fight in the ring. A touching little story. [PS/GS]

MADELEINE L'ENGLE
A Wrinkle in Time

A winner of the prestigious Newberry award, this exciting science fantasy novel has some underlying Christian themes. This volume is the first in a series. (See chapter eight for a further description.) [YA]

C. S. LEWIS
Chronicles of Narnia
(The Lion, the Witch, and the Wardrobe; Prince Caspian; The Voyage of the Dawn Treader;
The Silver Chair; The Magician's Nephew;
The Horse and His Boy; The Last Battle)
Letters to Children

The Chronicles of Narnia is a wonderful series of books that follows some children who find their way into the land of Narnia. They experience exciting adventures that teach them (and us) a great deal about redemption, salvation and the life of faith. Powerful theological insights are artfully cloaked in these delightful allegorical tales. Every child should be exposed to the spiritual and moral lessons taught in these classic books. Older children and adults will also gain much pleasure and insight from Lewis's Space trilogy and others of his many great books. [AA]

Children who enjoyed the Chronicles of Narnia will probably be interested in *Letters to Children*, which Lewis wrote in response to letters he received from children. Many of them discuss the meaning and origin of the Narnian tales. [YA]

ARNOLD LOBEL
Frog and Toad Are Friends

This wonderfully amusing collection of simple stories demonstrates the power of true friendship. [PS/GS]

HUGH LOFTING
Doctor Doolittle

The humorous adventures of a veterinarian who "talks with the animals."
[GS/YA]

JACK LONDON
Call of the Wild

This thrilling story chronicles the life of an arctic sled dog. It exposes the
thoughtless cruelty of humans and the reawakening of the dog's wild
nature. The intensity of the story makes it more suitable for older children.
[YA]

GEORGE MACDONALD
The Golden Key
The Princess and the Goblin
The Princess and Curdie
At the Back of the North Wind
Sir Gibbie

These books make good reading purely as fantasy-adventure stories, but
on a deeper level they are also powerful images of the spiritual life and the
path to spiritual maturity. *At the Back of the North Wind*, for example, is
helpful for children trying to come to terms with death. *Sir Gibbie*, one of
the most accessible of MacDonald's many novels, is written primarily for
adults, but will also be enjoyed by younger readers for its portrayal of an
orphan who learns about his magnificent and unexpected identity. [YA/
AA]

PATRICIA MACLACHLAN
Baby

A truly moving story about a family who finds an abandoned baby in the
driveway to their home with a note that says, "This is Sophie. She is almost
a year old and she is good. . . . I will come back for her one day. I love her."
So Larkin and her family learn to love Sophie as their own, knowing that
one day her mother will return. Sure to inspire some tears! [YA]

CATHERINE MARSHALL
Christy
A warm-hearted novel based on the true experiences of a young woman sent to teach in the Appalachian mountains in 1912, this is one of several fine books by Catherine Marshall. [YA]

ROBERT MCCLOSKEY
Make Way for Ducklings
A family of ducks faces the perils of city life. Very cute! [PS/GS]

HENRIETTA C. MEARS
What the Bible Is All About for Young Explorers
A great resource for helping children to better understand the Bible, this fine reference work contains overviews of each book of the Bible, themes, outlines and important background information. Parents be warned: You'll learn a lot too! [GS/YA]

A. A. MILNE
When We Were Very Young
Now We Are Six
Winnie the Pooh
The House at Pooh Corner
No child should grow up without a familiarity with the marvelous rhymes and poems contained in Milne's *When We Were Very Young* and *Now We Are Six*; they are charming, disarming and funny. Even more fun are the warm and humorous adventures of Winnie the Pooh and his friends, which are among my favorite books of all time. [AA]

LUCY MAUD MONTGOMERY
Anne of Green Gables
Instead of receiving the orphan boy that they had hoped for, a spinster brother and sister are sent young Anne by mistake. Anne's precocious imagination gets her into and out of a number of adventures. This is the first volume in a wonderful series. [YA]

MARY NORTON
The Borrowers

The adventures of tiny people who secretly live in (and borrow from) the homes of the regular-sized. Fun reading for kids. [YA]

KATHERINE PATERSON
Bridge to Terabithia
Jacob Have I Loved

Death is one of the hardest things for children to grasp. Paterson helps them come to terms with it in *Bridge to Teribithia*, a very emotionally stirring story about a girl who loses a dear friend. *Jacob Have I Loved* is a powerful examination of sibling rivalry and competitiveness. One of the best writers for young people, Paterson has written many other fine books worth investigating. [YA]

CHARLES PERRAULT
Fairy Tales
Mother Goose Rhymes

These are undisputed classics that all children are sure to love. [PS/GS]

WATTY PIPER
The Little Engine That Could

This charming tale teaches us that perseverance and hard work will pay off, as will a positive attitude toward the struggles that we face in life. [PS]

CHAIM POTOK
The Chosen

Older readers and listeners will gain much from this powerful novel about the physical, spiritual and intellectual coming of age of two young Jewish boys. A book full of rich insights and a valuable statement about tolerance. [YA]

BEATRIX POTTER
Peter Rabbit and Other Tales

Peter is an overly curious rabbit who disobeys his mother and almost gets caught by Mr. McGregor. Lovely illustrations highlight these simple tales. [PS/GS]

HOWARD PYLE
The Adventures of Robin Hood

The exciting tales of the man who stole from the rich to give to the poor. [YA]

H. A. REY
Curious George
Curious George Rides a Bike
Curious George Flies a Kite

George is a monkey who cannot keep himself out of trouble. He is, after much adventure, always rescued by his friend, the Man with the Yellow Hat. One of my very favorites! [PS/GS]

BARBARA ROBINSON
The Best Christmas Pageant Ever

The story of how the mean and unruly Herdman kids taught the rest of the church the true meaning of Christmas is a moving and fall-down funny book with a powerful message. [AA]

WILLIAM F. RUSSELL
Classic Myths to Read Aloud
Classics to Read Aloud to Your Children
More Classics to Read Aloud to Your Children

In *Classic Myths to Read Aloud* the Greek and Roman myths are revealed as a gold mine of moral instruction. Russell has written them at a level suitable for young children and has retained their mystery and dignity. These tales make effective discussion starters on moral issues. [GS/YA]

The collections of excerpts from the classics should serve to whet your children's appetites for great books. The entries are age-graded, with helpful introductions and vocabulary guides. [AA]

MAURICE SENDAK
Where the Wild Things Are

Some parents have found this book about friendly monsters to be an antidote to fear of nightmares. *There's a Nightmare in My Closet* by Mercer

Mayer is also good for this common problem. [PS/GS]

DOCTOR SEUSS
The Cat in the Hat
How the Grinch Stole Christmas
Horton Hears a Who

As a child I always had a special place in my heart for the stories of Dr. Seuss. Filled with nonsense and creativity, they make a good introduction to the pleasures of language. Many, like *Horton Hears a Who*, teach important lessons. The message "a person's a person, no matter how small" has special poignancy in this day of commonplace abortions. [PS/GS]

ANNA SEWELL
Black Beauty

A good story for girls and boys who love horses, as well as a passionate critique of cruelty to animals. [YA]

MARGERY SHARP
The Rescuers

An adventure story about the brave mice of the Prisoner's Aid Society, who help mice all over the world out of various troubles. [GS/YA]

ISAAC BASHEVIS SINGER
Children's Stories

The gifted Yiddish storyteller tells humorous and poignant tales, including the classic story of loyalty, "Zlateh the Goat." [AA]

ESPHYR SLOBODKINA
Caps for Sale

The adventures of a hat peddler whose caps are stolen by mischievous monkeys. [PS/GS]

PATRICIA ST. JOHN
Treasures in the Snow

When her little brother is crippled by the town bully, Annette sets out to gain revenge and learns about anger, hatred and forgiveness. This and other St. John books are distinguished by powerful Christian messages. [YA]

WILLIAM STEIG
Yellow and Pink

This very funny little parable makes a powerful argument that humans are the creation of God, not the result of chance or purposeless evolution. Very subtle, but very profound. [GS/AA]

ROBERT LOUIS STEVENSON
A Child's Garden of Verses
Treasure Island

Children of many generations have treasured the simple poems of *A Child's Garden of Verses,* which makes wonderful bedtime reading. *Treasure Island,* a classic pirate tale, is sure to delight most young shipmates! I can remember listening breathlessly to this book as a child, captivated by its exciting plot twists and turns. [AA/YA]

ADRIEN STOUTENBURG
American Tall Tales

The stories of Paul Bunyan, Pecos Bill, Davy Crockett, Johnny Appleseed and others stretch our imaginations and our credulity. [GS/YA]

ROSEMARY SUTCLIFF
The Sword and the Circle

Brilliant, well-written retellings of Arthurian Britain and the knights of the round table. [YA]

JONATHAN SWIFT
Gulliver's Travels

Profound and humorous insights into human nature are gained through the eyes of the intrepid traveler, Gulliver. Parts of this book are suitable for children; other sections are best left for young adults. [YA]

CORRIE TEN BOOM
The Hiding Place

The heroic true story of Corrie Ten Boom and her sister depicts the hardships of a Nazi concentration camp, which they endured by the strength of their faith and trust in God. Though intense in its depiction of evil, the triumph of righteousness makes this very worthwhile reading for adults and children alike. [YA]

J. R. R. TOLKIEN
The Hobbit
The Lord of the Rings *(The Fellowship of the Ring; The Two*
Towers; The Return of the King)
Farmer Giles of Ham

Tolkien's stories celebrate heroism and an appreciation for the simple things of life. These tales of the battle between good and evil will excite the listener and challenge the imagination. Tolkien's Christian worldview shows through in subtle and powerful ways. *The Hobbit* and *Farmer Giles* are appropriate for younger children, but The Lord of the Rings is more sophisticated, very demanding and possibly somewhat frightening for the very young. [YA]

MARK TWAIN
The Adventures of Tom Sawyer
The Adventures of Huckleberry Finn

These books are among the most entertaining in the English language. You'll laugh and thrill to the adventures of these two intrepid explorers. The entire family will be sure to enjoy these Twain classics. [YA/AA]

JUDITH VIORST
Alexander and the Terrible, Horrible, No Good, Very Bad Day

A very funny book that kids and adults will immediately be able to relate to. Alexander has one of those days when everything seems to go wrong, and we find ourselves feeling both empathetic and amused. A good book for teaching us not to take ourselves too seriously, it can help turn a bad day around and bring a smile to the face of even the most grumpy. [PS/GS]

CYNTHIA VOIGHT
Homecoming

Great plotting and wonderful characters mark this first book in a strong series about the Tillerman family, who live in a small town on Chesapeake Bay. [YA]

WALTER WANGERIN
The Book of the Dun Cow
Potter

Wangerin is a contemporary Christian writer of abundant insight and writing talent. His vocabulary can be challenging at times, but your children will find him worth the effort. [YA]

ROSEMARY WELLS
Morris's Disappearing Bag

In this one of the many slyly amusing stories by Rosemary Wells, Morris gets back at his big sisters and brother who tell him that he is too little to play with their toys. [GS]

E. B. WHITE
Charlotte's Web

This wise and eloquent story about the friendship between a pig and a spider is one of the most popular of modern children's stories. White's prose is a model of good writing. [GS/AA]

LAURA INGALLS WILDER
Little House on the Prairie series

The nine books of the Little House series are based on the author's prairie childhood. They reflect a family lifestyle based on Christian values, hard work, and mutual love and respect. Your children will see moral virtue in action in this fine and unforgettable set of books. They are wonderful for reading aloud; begin with *Little House in the Big Woods*. [GS/AA]

MARGERY WILLIAMS
The Velveteen Rabbit

A children's classic, this is the beautiful story about a stuffed animal who becomes real through the love of his young owner. [GS/AA]

GENE ZION
Harry the Dirty Dog

A great story for kids who balk at having to take a bath. [PS/GS]

Ten

How to Make Use of These Reading Lists

One of the values of lists such as those in this book is that they provide valuable suggestions on which books are worth buying in order to build a personal library of real quality. Many of these books are available in a variety of editions, ranging from the dog-eared used paperback to exquisite leather editions, finely crafted and sturdily bound. Whether your pocketbook dictates frugality or allows prodigality in your spending on books, such books will be a lasting resource and an intellectual and spiritual treasure. And they are the best of investments in terms of helping you to store up lasting riches of the kind that really matter.

I often refer to my personal library, large and ever expanding, as my "adjacent brain." It is a storehouse for ideas and information, the sum of which I could never manage to stuff into my own cranial cavity. But though I cannot readily draw all this information from my head, it is always as close as my bookshelves. Countless wonders, intriguing ideas, infuriating arguments, paradoxical puzzles, soul-stirring stories, empirical facts and spiritual resources are all stored on my shelves, and the reach of my hand can bring any of them within my grasp.

But these riches are lost to me if they remain trapped within the covers of unread books. It is not enough simply to own books. They are not meant to be merely looked at, but to be looked into. If we do not read the books we own, we are like the farmer who owned the land over a large reserve of oil buried deep in the ground, but who lived in a tumbledown shanty in ignorance of his potential wealth because he never made the effort to drill on his land.

Unfortunately, many people get the idea that once they are finished with school they are also finished with serious reading, with study and with learning. For many people, the completion of their formal education marks the end of reading as anything other than a leisure pursuit for entertainment. They see reading as an activity akin to watching television—a way to relax and unwind. Books that challenge and require careful reading do not fit this function. Thus, the primary reading material of many Christians is the most predictable sort of fiction or feel-good inspirational writing.

There is nothing wrong with reading for entertainment. That is certainly one of its valid functions, and a noble one at that, because many of the very greatest books are extremely entertaining. But people who read *only* for entertainment are robbing themselves of one of the true pleasures of reading: that of expanding the mind, the heart, the soul and the spirit.

Learning does not and should not cease with the end of formal education. Learning is a lifelong activity. God created us to be earnest seekers after the truth our whole lives; when we stop learning, we stop growing.

Setting Personal Goals

If we are to seek continued learning, we will have much greater success if we discipline ourselves to bring some kind of plan or structure to this activity. If we do not discipline ourselves and make time for expanding our knowledge and understanding, it is unlikely that real learning will take place. Our lives are simply too busy, too filled with activity to have a catch-as-catch-can attitude toward the acquiring of knowledge and wisdom. We need some sort of plan. If it is not important enough to us to set goals and make thoughtful choices in our reading, we will probably not find the time for serious, focused study. On the other hand, if we do set some achievable and worthwhile goals, we stand to gain much.

One summer while I was still in college, I realized that my knowledge of the Greek and Roman classics was spotty at best, and I decided to focus some of my reading during the summer break on these books. Since I worked afternoons and my wife worked mornings, I had an hour or so every day (after tending to our newborn and cleaning around the apartment) to dedicate to reading. That summer I read Homer's *The Odyssey*, several plays by the major Greek playwrights (Aeschylus, Aristophanes, Sophocles and Euripides), Virgil's *The Aeneid* and Plutarch's *Lives of the Noble Greeks and Romans*, as well as a couple of Plato's dialogues and a smattering of Aristotle. Looking back on that summer, it is amazing how much I read and absorbed during those three months. I didn't look forward to going back to school again because I was afraid it would get in the way of my education!

To this day I always try to spend some of my reading time in the classics. Since I always have several books going at once, one is usually a classic, one a work of philosophy or theology, one a devotional classic (for the early mornings) and one a novel. Which I turn to depends on my mood or my discipline. I try to vary my reading between fiction and nonfiction, throwing in an occasional book of poetry. If I'm trying to become informed on a particular subject, I often read a number of related books, one after the other.

I try to finish every book I begin. Sometimes, while forcing my way through a book that is failing to arouse my deepest interest, I will run across a passage that will stop me in my tracks and leave me reeling with its insight.

Life is too short not to fill some of the quiet hours with rich reading experiences. I have learned to make time and to make sacrifices to bring the insights of some of the most profound men and women into my life through reading quality books.

You may want to start with the cream of the crop, with those books that should be a part of every Christian's "mental furniture." I have created a list of ten books that will make a very good starting place for your personal reading plan. All of these books have influenced the lives of countless numbers of people throughout history. None of them requires any special knowledge or vocabulary to read with understanding, and all are addressed to the average person, not primarily the theologian or expert. After reading these, you can branch out to explore other classic works.

Ten Books That Every Christian Ought to Know

1. *Confessions,* Augustine
2. *The Divine Comedy,* Dante
3. *The Imitation of Christ,* Thomas à Kempis
4. *The Practice of the Presence of God,* Brother Lawrence
5. *Pensées,* Blaise Pascal
6. *The Pilgrim's Progress,* John Bunyan
7. *The Brothers Karamazov,* Fyodor Dostoyevsky
8. *The Pursuit of God,* A. W. Tozer
9. *Mere Christianity,* C. S. Lewis
10. *Celebration of Discipline,* Richard Foster

Ten Books to Help You Develop a Christian Worldview

1. *Mere Christianity,* C. S. Lewis
2. *Orthodoxy,* G. K. Chesterton
3. *More Than a Carpenter,* Josh McDowell
4. *The Universe Next Door,* James Sire
5. *Scaling the Secular City,* J. P. Moreland
6. *Knowing God,* J. I. Packer
7. *Christianity for Modern Pagans,* Peter J. Kreeft
8. *Essentials of Evangelical Theology,* Donald Bloesch
9. *How Now Shall We Live?* Charles Colson
10. *Loving God,* Charles Colson

Ten Authors Who Will Help You Reflect More Deeply on Being a Christian in the Modern World

1. C. S. Lewis
2. Francis Schaeffer
3. Os Guinness
4. Paul Johnson
5. Philip Yancey
6. Alasdair MacIntyre
7. Reinhold Niebuhr
8. Lesslie Newbigin
9. Walker Percy
10. Ravi Zacharias

Ten Poets Whose Work Demonstrates the Beauty of the Christian View of the World

1. George Herbert
2. T. S. Eliot
3. John Donne
4. Thomas Traherne
5. Gerard Manley Hopkins
6. Luci Shaw
7. Robert Browning
8. Kelly Cherry
9. William Shakespeare
10. John Milton

Ten of My Favorite Novels

1. *The Brothers Karamazov,* Fyodor Dostoyevsky
2. *A Soldier of the Great War,* Mark Helprin
3. *Anna Karenina,* Leo Tolstoy
4. *Les Miserables,* Victor Hugo
5. *Jane Eyre,* Charlotte Brontë
6. *The Brothers K,* James David Duncan
7. *The Adventures of Huckleberry Finn,* Mark Twain
8. *The Power and the Glory,* Graham Greene
9. *The Second Coming,* Walker Percy
10. *Cancer Ward,* Alexander Solzhenitsyn

Now it's up to you . . . have fun exploring!

ELEVEN

THE JOY OF READING GROUPS

A s wonderful as the experience of solitary reading and study can be, there is nothing that can compare with the excitement and fun of discussing books we have read with other people who have a similar love for books and reading. Of course, this can and does happen in the most natural ways. On a recent plane trip I was reading Kurt Vonnegut's anti-utopian novel, *Player Piano*. One of the flight attendants, who had recently read the book, saw me reading it and struck up an enjoyable conversation. I have had similar experiences innumerable times. Isn't it part of human nature that we like to talk with others about experiences we have in common, whether it is last Sunday's football game, a particularly good movie, a favorite television program or a good book? Instantly, we have the grounds for an interesting conversation.

Many people have found that such conversations are too good to be left to chance and have formed reading groups with the express purpose of reading and discussing good books. Discussing books with others helps you to cement themes in your mind, to garner new insights and to share with others the pleasure derived from a truly memorable book.

Discussions in reading groups are similar to the construction of a quilt. Everyone brings his or her own personal insights from a book read in common and shares them with the group. Others see things that you missed or failed to appreciate. Each of us has a unique pattern of understanding and interpreting the books we read, because each of us draws from a unique fund of experiences and knowledge. We each bring our own "square" before the assembled group, and what emerges is a beautiful quilt of enriched understanding. Our own thoughts are stitched together with those of others to form a bigger, fuller, broader appreciation. The quilt takes shape before our eyes in the process of discussion. We see something bigger than we could see when we were limited to our own pair of eyes and our single brain.

This process challenges us to think clearly about the message and meaning of the book under discussion so that we can better articulate it to the others in the group. This encourages us to become more careful readers.

One of the wondrous things that can happen is one member of the group helping others to truly appreciate the riches of a book they didn't fully understand. I was called on to lead a discussion of Dostoyevsky's *Crime and Punishment* for a group I belong to. The majority of those who attended that night had found the book puzzling and a bit tedious. Many failed to enjoy the book or derive much insight from it. But as I brought insights and favorite passages before the group during the course of the evening, a palpable change took place. Suddenly, the book began to make sense to them, and they connected some of their own insights with mine. By the end of the discussion, I had won most of the group over to it. My own connection with and enthusiasm for the book was infectious. Many commented afterward that they left with an appreciation for Dostoyevsky's profound insight into human nature that they had not had at the beginning of the evening.

At other times, I have been on the receiving side of such a discussion, where others have opened up a book for me that I had failed to truly appreciate. It is a glorious demonstration of how the body of Christ can function, even in the reading of a book. Everyone can bring out something that others have not seen and thereby create a fuller understanding for the group as a whole.

The group I belong to currently has about twenty members, with an average turnout of five to fifteen people at any one session. We meet once a month to talk about the book we have all been reading in common during the previous month. Several have said that the group provides them with the discipline to read many great books they might not otherwise find the time to read. We laugh a lot. Sometimes we raise our voices in disagreement. Often we share deeply personal experiences that are brought to mind because of the themes of the book.

We emphasize variety in our readings. We have read contemporary novels like *Prince of Tides* (Pat Conroy), *A River Runs Through It* (Norman MacLean), *Godric* (Frederick Buechner), *Father Melancholy's Daughter* (Gail Godwin), *The Second Coming* (Walker Percy) and *This House of Sky* (Ivan Doig). We've read such nonfiction as *Lincoln at Gettysburg* (Gary Wills), the autobiographical memoir *Days of Grace* (Arthur Ashe), *West with the Night* (Beryl Markham) and the epic Civil War history *Battle Cry of Freedom* (James McPherson). We have also discussed children's books such as *Anne of Green Gables* (Lucy Maud Montgomery) and *The Wind in the Willows* (Kenneth Grahame). A number of Christian classics have also made their way onto our list: *Surprised by Joy* (C. S. Lewis), *Pensées* (Blaise Pascal), *The Pilgrim's Progress* (John Bunyan) and *The Imitation of Christ* (Thomas à Kempis).

Many of our very best discussions have come from the classics—memorable books like *Jane Eyre* (Charlotte Brontë), *Frankenstein* (Mary Shelley), *A Farewell to Arms* (Ernest Hemingway) and *The Merchant of Venice* (Shakespeare). We had a particularly rich experience on a summer evening when we met in the park to share favorite poems by Hopkins, Blake, Wordsworth, Dickinson and others.

One of the most valuable things about reading in groups is the discipline it gives you to get through at least one significant book each month. And a reading group will introduce you to many fine authors whose works you'll want to explore on your own. I was so entranced by J. R. R. Tolkien's *The Fellowship of the Ring* that within that year I went on to read everything else he had written.

Over the years, I have belonged to several different reading groups. I was still in college when the first of these groups was begun—by the woman who was to become my wife. The group was not only where she and I met but also where we learned of common interests we had in the realms of both books and life. Another group was dedicated to discussing the works of C. S. Lewis and the other Inklings (Lewis's colleagues from Oxford). A third group, made up primarily of clergy and college professors, read academic works in philosophy and theology. The variety of theological perspectives made for particularly vigorous discussion. I strongly encourage you to join or start a group for people who want to read and discuss good books. It is not only intellectually invigorating, it is also immensely enjoyable.

Churches would do well to encourage their members to start small reading groups made up of church members. They might, for example, read some of the books from "The Great Books of the Christian Tradition" list. Imagine how such reading, held in common, could raise the level of understanding and communication in your fellowship.

Members might also consider that such groups could be a very effective form of evangelism. Nonbelievers who attend can be introduced to a Christian vision of reality in a very nonthreatening and open atmosphere. By reading the right kinds of books, you open people up to consideration of the most fundamental human questions: questions about God, suffering, evil, human nature, redemption and change. I believe that quality modern fiction can be one of the most powerful ways to open people's hearts to those questions that are only fully answered in the hope of the gospel. You'll get an idea for the variety available by perusing chapter eight. However, keep in mind that most of these books are not written from a Christian perspective. Some of these books raise the questions only to suggest the wrong answers, but they still do the service of provoking good discussions of important issues. Make sure you have mature Christians in the group to introduce the answers that arise out of the Christian worldview.

Finally, here are a few tips on making your group successful.

☐ Most groups find that meeting once a month is about the right frequency. A month gives people plenty of time to obtain the book and finish the reading. If the meeting is at a regular time (the first Friday of every month, for example), it is easier for members to plan their schedules around it and keep track of the date.

☐ Keep the group small. Fifteen is about as many as you can accommodate and still have the feeling of intimacy and the opportunity for everyone to have a say. Having too many people seems to raise inhibitions and stifle discussion.

☐ Have a facilitator, not a teacher. This is no place for a lecture, and no one person should dominate the group. You need someone to start the discussion and keep it moving, but this person should allow the discussion to take on a life of its own. The goal is not to find the "correct interpretation" of the book, but rather to discuss and have fellowship around the book and its themes. In all the groups I have belonged to, the various members have shared the duty of leading, taking turns in some sort of informal rotation.

☐ The discussion leader should attempt as much as possible to draw everyone into the discussion. In any group there are likely to be those who will dominate the conversation if they are allowed to. The seasoned leader will learn to engage everyone. I have learned that a valuable discussion technique is to pose a question on which everyone in the room can give their opinion. For instance, during a discussion of *Anne of Green Gables*, the following question was posed: Would you rather be thought beautiful, clever or good? The responses as the inquiry made its way around the room stimulated many interesting comments. The leader should also be aware that some people are simply not very willing to express their opinions aloud. Do not try to force these reticent ones. Over time their level of confidence will grow, or they will read a book that so affects them that they cannot keep silent.

☐ The discussion leader should do some background study on the author. Sometimes the events of an author's life help to bring insight into his or her writing and provide a context for understanding and appreciating the work at hand. When I have been the leader and time has allowed, I have read a brief biography of the author prior to the meeting, or other works that might shed light on the book under discussion. If you choose to do this, it is important to keep your remarks short, maybe five to ten minutes. Remember, this is not a lecture. If you present yourself as an expert on this book or author, it can intimidate other group members, causing them to feel a lack of confidence that their comments are worth being heard. Nothing damages the spirit of a reading group faster than a know-it-all windbag!

☐ The group I currently belong to sends out a short letter prior to each meeting reminding members of the time, date, place and book that we are reading. The letter also has a few questions drawn up by the discussion leader to help us begin thinking about some of the important issues in the book.

□ Serving a light snack or refreshments helps to give the meeting an informal and relaxed feeling. Perhaps different members of the group can take turns providing cookies, cheese and crackers, vegetables and dip, or some other snack food. For reasons that I cannot fully explain, the availability of food seems to relax people and put them in a proper mood for discussion.

These few suggestions should be enough to help you get a group started. Even three or four interested readers should be adequate to begin with, and the riches you will gain from participation in such a group are extraordinary. Join the adventure!

APPENDIX A

DISCOVERING OUR CHRISTIAN HERITAGE

The only palliative [for the errors of our modern world]
is to keep the clean sea breeze of the centuries blowing through our minds,
and this can be done only by reading old books.
Not, of course, that there is any magic about the past.
People were no cleverer than they are now;
they made as many mistakes as we.
But not the same mistakes.
C. S. LEWIS

I'll never forget her distraught face as she sat in my office. When Sharon had first entered college, she was a bright and enthusiastic Christian. Now, almost four years later, her faith was more timid and less self-assured. Though she still hung on to the emotional comforts of her beliefs, she had given up trying to integrate them with her intellectual pursuits. In the world of academia her belief system seemed quaint somehow, irrelevant and old-fashioned. Her evangelical commitment was, her professors told her, just one of many options from which to choose in order to build an intellectual framework for thinking—and an out-of-date one at that!

What Sharon had failed to understand before she entered college is that the Christian faith is not just some unique modern way of looking at life, but the single most powerful influence in the construction of Western civilization. Her professors had neglected, out of ignorance or prejudice, to point out the vital impact that a personal faith had on many of the greatest artists, writers and thinkers of our culture. She also had failed to understand this truth: Christianity is not just a modern conservative outlook on life, but a richly textured way of looking at life and understanding our existence as human beings. Sharon, like so many other Christian young people, had become intellectually timid about her faith, suffering an embarrassment that arose primarily because she was not aware of the richness and diversity of the Christian tradition. If we have an awareness of our heritage as believers, it can give us a sense of confidence and pride in the face of a secularism that dismisses our faith as an empty passing fad.

Our lives will not be well nourished by an exclusive diet of the new and trendy. To truly grow intellectually and spiritually, to break outside the limitations of our own modern patterns of thought, requires that we partake of the rich feast that is part of our past.

To think in this way goes against the grain of much modern thinking. Tradition has a bad name in our society and often in evangelical circles as well. When many people think of tradition, it conjures up the specter of mindlessly following old and antiquated ways. They view it as an exterminator of spontaneity, a shallow and lifeless substitution of yesterday's belief for today's practice. I do not believe that this way of thinking about tradition does justice to the biblical view, which stresses the importance of handing down the riches of our faith. To teach our children to appreciate our Christian heritage and to drink deeply at the wells of tradition is an important part of our task as parents and educators.

In the Old Testament we see the importance of faith as a tradition, a heritage passed down from generation to generation. In Deuteronomy 6 when Moses was given commandments for the people of God, parents were instructed to teach these commandments to their children and to pass them on to subsequent generations. And not only the commandments themselves were to be taught but also the story of God's dealings with his people.

Some mistakenly believe that Jesus completely condemned all tradition. They will point to passages like Mark 7:8-9 or Matthew 15:3 to demonstrate the supposed negative attitude that Jesus held toward tradition. But a careful reading of these passages will clarify that it is not tradition itself that Jesus condemned, only false and shallow tradition. He frowned on the kind of tradition that exalts itself above the commands of God and replaces religion of the heart with empty and lifeless formulas. This kind of tradition harbors itself in the past without due appreciation for what God is doing in the present or will do in the future. It idolizes the past but does not realize that the past is primarily valuable to us because it teaches us how to live in the present.

Many fail to comprehend the difference between tradition and traditionalism. Jaroslav Pelikan articulately differentiates between the two: Tradition is "the living faith of the dead," which can still affect us in positive ways, nurturing and challenging us, and traditionalism is "the dead faith of the living," which holds onto the outward rituals and rhetoric of belief but does not burn with an inner fire of passion for God. Ultimately, tradition in the church is the ongoing, living influence of the Holy Spirit. Because God is alive and his Spirit is alive, the truth renews itself on a continual basis. It is ever fresh. But at the same time the truth is ever the same; it does not change. We do not look for new truth but for the truth to constantly make itself heard anew. Simone Weil reminds us that "to be always relevant, you have to say things which are eternal."

Tradition tells us that we need to be attentive to the past and to what we can learn from it. According to G. K. Chesterton, tradition is the important task of learning from the wisdom of those who have gone before us:

> Tradition may be defined as an extension of the franchise. Tradition means giving votes to the most obscure of all classes, our ancestors. It is the democracy of the dead. Tradition refuses to submit to the small and arrogant oligarchy of those who merely happen to be walking about. (*Orthodoxy*)

Some will argue, of course, that we do not need to listen to the voice of the past but only need to hear God in the present. But such a dismissive attitude toward the richness of our heritage may be, at its root, a spiritual problem. It may indicate an arrogant pride in ourselves and our own resources. I can remember as a young Christian being counseled by an older believer against reading Bible commentaries and works of theology because, I was told, all I really needed was the Bible itself; all that I needed to know could be drawn from its pages. This idea troubled me for some time, causing me to feel guilty for reading anything other than the Scriptures. But I slowly came to realize the hidden arrogance of believing that I did not need the insights and revelations of those who had preceded me. To suggest that I would be harmed by the insights of brilliant and godly women and men of the past and present seems an ignorant and truly dangerous folly. Are not all believers part of the body of Christ? And is that body not extended over time as well as space? Do we not need each other? Are our ancestors in the faith not of any importance to us today?

The philosopher Leo Strauss has pointed out that in any one generation there is only a handful of truly great minds. This means that if our minds are to be instructed by the most insightful of human thinkers, this learning must take place primarily through the instrument of books. In great books we encounter great minds.

Further, we should not make the error of supposing that tradition is the same as conformity. In considering the importance of tradition, we are not talking about a thoughtless following of past ways and ideas. Instead, what we must understand is that our contemporary work is part of a succession from the past and that we function best in the present when we take the past into account. We do not need to reinvent the wheel in each generation. Can you imagine how slowly science would progress if each and every scientist had to go back to the beginning and rediscover the basic laws of science for himself or herself? Instead, scientists build on the work of those who have gone before them, as we do in every area of our lives every day.

Bernardus of Silvestris, a twelfth-century monk, wrote regarding the successes of his own day: "We see farther because we stand on the shoulders of giants." So it is for us. As believers we stand on the shoulders of the likes of Augustine, Aquinas, Luther, Calvin and Jonathan Edwards. We can build on their insights and use their perspectives as a vantage point to critique our own time. Sometimes it is difficult to see our own cultural attitudes and ideas clearly and objectively because they are so much a part of us. We take them for granted, accept them without the critical examination they need to undergo. But from the vantage point of a former time and place, gained through attentive reading of the classics of our tradition, we can see how time-bound and ungodly some of our own cherished prejudices really are. T. S. Eliot writes, "Someone has said: 'The dead writers are remote from us because we know so much more than they did.' Precisely, and they are that which we know" (*The Sacred Wood*).

There is a widespread belief in our culture that our present time is so progressive that we no longer have need of our "barbaric" past. The fact that we are progressing is easy to see in the realm of technology and machinery. I have seen, in my own lifetime, rapid changes and transformations in many kinds of technology. What was once only the stuff of fantastic dreams has become a reality, and we are so used to them that they are now almost humdrum. Unfortunately, the concept of a constant progression of improvement that leaves the past behind has carried over into the realm of human thought and morals. We tend to see what is more recent as more enlightened than what preceded it. C. S. Lewis labels this kind of thinking "chronological snobbery." Lewis writes in his autobiography about how his friend Owen Barfield questioned his youthful trust in the merely contemporary, and how he was cured of this attitude:

> Barfield . . . made short work of what I have called my "chronological snobbery," the uncritical acceptance of the intellectual climate common to our age and the assumption that whatever has gone out of date is on that account discredited. You must find out why it went out of date; was it ever refuted (and if so by whom, where and how conclusively) or did it merely die away as fashions do? If the latter, this tells us nothing about its truth or falsehood. From seeing this one passes to the realization that our age is also a "period," and certainly has, like all periods, its own characteristic illusions. They are likeliest to lurk in those widespread assumptions which are so ingrained in the age that no one dares to attack or feels it necessary to defend them. (*Surprised by Joy*)

Lewis believed that the myth of progress was a powerfully motivating force in our modern world. In his essay "The Funeral of a Great Myth" Lewis draws a distinction between the scientific theory of evolution and the popular idea of evolution as progressive improvement in all areas of existence. The result of this myth of constant progress is to cause us to place great (and unwarranted) trust in our present understandings. Instead of looking to Aristotle or Aquinas for a moral theory, we concentrate on the latest prognostications of the social-science pundits. Consequently, we treat the thinking of the past as irrelevant, thereby cutting ourselves off from its riches. Severed from tradition, we rob ourselves of a source that would provide us with a standpoint from which we can critique our own age.

For what tradition does for us is free us from the siren song of relevancy. All the voices around us seem to be crying out the importance of making education "relevant." Unfortunately, what this usually means is making ourselves slaves of the contemporary, following the pied piper of the latest trend or fad. We use our perceived freedom from the constraints of the past to follow blindly the whims of the moment. We are busily trying to catch the next wave of innovation. But as Dean Inge wrote, "He who is married to the spirit of the age will soon find himself a widower." While the "relevant" is ever shifting and changing, the truths embedded in tradition remain constant.

Tradition is also a fountainhead of creativity. Paradoxically, the work of artists and thinkers who immersed themselves most in the traditions of the past are among the most creative. Pablo Picasso, T. S. Eliot and James Joyce all made striking innovations in their fields. All of them were patient students of the traditions out of which their art arose.

The past is a priceless treasure. We need to recapture a sense of our place in the unfolding of God's plan for the ages and an appreciation for the "communion of saints"—the contribution of believers throughout time. Thomas Oden, a theologian who spent much of his early theological career focused on the latest cultural and theological whims, has increasingly become committed to the importance of the writings of the early church. "Once hesitant to trust anyone over thirty," he writes, "now I hesitate to trust anyone under three hundred." Oden bemoans the lack of historical perspective he sees in the modern church:

> We need to recover a sense of the active work of the Spirit in history, through living communities. Our modern individualism too easily tempts us to take our Bible and remove ourselves from the wider believing community. We end up with a Bible and a radio, but no church. (As quoted in *No God but God*)

We need to reacquaint ourselves with the riches of our Christian heritage. I hope this book can help people in that process. We will find our lives greatly enriched as we read the great books of the Christian tradition, study them in groups, pass them around in our churches and teach their ideas to our children. I think we'll find that sometimes we can gain a startlingly new perspective from that which we might be tempted to label as old.

Appendix B

Plundering the Egyptians

Why Read Books by Non-Christians?

I remember as a teenager being advised by a well-meaning older believer that I should "shy away from reading books by pagans and atheists." I'm sure his concern was for my spiritual growth. After all, I was a teenager and was poised at some crossroads in my life at that impressionable age. He didn't want me to be led down the path toward secularism or have my mind sullied with inappropriate language or wrong teachings. Instead, he recommended that, as much as possible, I only read books by Christian writers.

For a time, I took his advice. I worried that maybe he was right—that God would be displeased with me if I spent time reading books by people who had rejected him. And wasn't part of the fundamentalist teaching I was exposed to every Sunday morning that there was a great gulf between the sacred and the secular? Wouldn't the true followers of Christ stand out by what they stood against? Thankfully, another older and wiser believer helped me to see that though my friend's heart was in the right place, his advice was misguided. By shutting myself off from the words of the "worldly," I was also shutting myself off from one of the channels by which I might come to know God and his ways more clearly.

It isn't hard to see how one might arrive at a position of thinking it necessary to protect oneself from ungodly thinking at all costs. Let's face it: we live in confusing and challenging times. Many key facets of Christian belief, once widely accepted and unquestioned, are now under attack. Where Christianity once earned at least a grudging respect, now many seek to discredit it. In the world of higher education, God is usually considered irrelevant to the task of better understanding. The idea that faith can help us discover truth is rejected out of hand. Instead, we are told that truth is relative and subjective, not objective and absolute. Thus, the very concept of truth itself is under vigorous attack.

It isn't surprising then that this has given birth to an attitude of defensiveness among many believers, who label all but explicitly Christian writing as dangerous or unworthy of the attention of the faithful. Hence, the writings of some of the greatest minds of all time, and the insights of some of our most penetrating modern thinkers, are dismissed as unworthy of consideration by believers. In what we have come to envision as a cultural "war," there is no room for harboring the thoughts and ideas of our adversaries. Instead, we must create our own alternative intellectual structure, our own subculture. And we have largely succeeded at doing just that.

We have Christian music, Christian bookstores, Christian television and Christian schools, and use the word *Christian* as a modifier for many other categories. But when we do this, we face the grave danger of devaluing all that does not specifically wear the label Christian. When we separate ourselves to this extent, we lose our impact on the culture at large and deprive ourselves of the insights we could draw from those whose faith or worldview is different than ours.

Such an attitude is not only intellectually foolhardy; it is also bad theology.

Two Types of Revelation

There is a misguided form of Christian thinking that draws a sharp distinction between the earthly and heavenly spheres, dismissing the things of earth as unimportant. But this kind of attitude does not rise from a proper understanding of biblical Christianity but, rather, a form of Gnosticism or Neoplatonism. Biblical faith values all that God created and believes that he is working out his purposes within the earthly sphere. Therefore, everything that concerns us as earthbound human beings also concerns God. When God became human in the person of Jesus Christ, his act forever sanctified what it means to be human. And so the human, earthly sphere of existence is never to be dismissed or taken lightly. If it was good enough for the Creator, who pronounced it so at creation, it should be good enough for us. God is not just concerned about spiritual matters. All of his creation is important. We should beware of the attitude of trying to be more spiritual than God!

Theologians differentiate between two types of revelation, and it is here, perhaps, that the misunderstandings lie. The first is *general revelation* and is available to all people everywhere. The glories of nature, the innate moral law within us and the logic of the created order are all sources that reveal something of God to us. These same sources are the basis for understanding God's created world. The second form of revelation is *special revelation*. Its primary focus is the revelation of God in the person of Jesus Christ, but it also includes the inspired record of God's dealings with his people, the Bible. Thomas Aquinas called these two forms of revelation "God's two books."

As believers we give a definite priority to special revelation, especially where it instructs us about the things of God. Where general revelation is often vague and cloudy (note the confusion found in humanly made religions based on general revelation), the special revelation of Scripture is quite clear in the essential elements of humankind's redemption and relationship with God. Therefore, we should focus our attention *primarily* on the Scriptures if we desire to be instructed in matters of theology and personal holiness.

When we turn to matters of science, history and medicine, however, it is not such a simple matter. Here we are struck by the limitations of special revelation. Though it does indeed make some statements about these areas (and when it does, we must listen attentively), it does not speak of them in detail or use the terminology of these various disciplines. In such areas, the Bible speaks truly, but not exhaustively. This means that we must turn to the data of general revelation to complete our knowledge. For example, the Bible is quite clear that God is the creator of the cosmos, but we are given few details on how the creative act was accomplished. Likewise, the Bible says nothing about the intricacies of quantum physics, medical science, botany or geology. This should not be interpreted as a shortcoming in the Bible; the dispensing of this kind of information is not its purpose.

God has "written" another book to provide us with this kind of information: general revelation. When the Bible speaks, we must heed its authoritative words. Where it is silent, we are called to use our God-given faculties of reason and creativity to experiment, inquire and explore the book of nature. Because the two "books" have the same author, when they both speak on a topic, they will, ultimately, never contradict each other. If we think we see a contradiction, it is apparent rather than real. Either (1) we have misunderstood Scripture, not properly interpreting its meaning, or (2) we have misunderstood the evidence of nature and have given it an incorrect interpretation. The truths of science and Scripture will never conflict. Only our false interpretations of one or the other will cause an apparent disagreement.

The Biblical Teaching on General Revelation

The Bible indicates that we can learn a great deal if we attend carefully to the world God created. Psalm 19 points to two sources that can instruct us in the power and majesty of God: the book of nature (verses 1-6) and the book of the law (verses 7-14). Both Scripture and the created order speak to us of God's character:

> The heavens declare the glory of God;
>   the skies proclaim the work of his hands.
> Day after day they pour forth speech;
>   night after night they display knowledge.
> There is no speech or language
>   where their voice is not heard.
> Their voice goes out into all the earth,
>   their words to the ends of the world. (Psalm 19:1-4)

If we train ourselves to attentiveness, having "ears to hear," nature itself can speak to us of the truth. Romans 1:18-32 offers a similar acknowledgment of nature's revelation: "For since the creation of the world God's invisible qualities—his eternal power and divine nature—have been clearly seen, being understood from what has been made, so that men are without excuse" (verse 20). Of course, as Paul points out, this knowledge has most often been ignored or perverted by sinful human beings. This is why we need the special revelation of God in Christ and the Word of God; the knowledge we gain from general revelation is not enough to save us, only enough to make us realize our predicament.

We can see further evidence of this balance between the sacred and the secular in Paul's life and ministry. There are at least two clear instances in which Paul appealed to knowledge outside special revelation. In Acts 14:15-17, Paul and Barnabas were preaching in Lystra. When the people of the city mistook Paul and Barnabas for gods and wanted to sacrifice to them, Paul rebuked them, assuring them that he and Barnabas were not divine. However, Paul points out that they have no excuse for ignorance of the living God, for "he has not left himself without testimony" (14:17). Here Paul was speaking not to Jews but to Greeks. He indicated that they could have some knowledge of the true God even though they had not been recipients of special revelation.

In Acts 17:22-31, Paul was preaching to the Greeks again, this time in Athens. When he saw that they had constructed an altar to "AN UNKNOWN GOD," he used it as an opportunity to draw a connection between what they knew and the good news of the gospel. The God that they had not known is the God whom Paul reveals to them. In making his case, Paul does something interesting, something important to the point of this chapter: In verse 28 he quotes one of their own pagan poets as a familiar and accurate source of information. Paul was not afraid to use secular sources when those sources spoke the truth. He could do this because he was committed to the idea that all truth is God's truth. There is no such thing as Christian truth as opposed to non-Christian truth.

General Revelation in the Christian Tradition

Because all truth is God's truth, the early Christian theologian Justin Martyr could write, "Whatever has been well said anywhere or by anyone belongs to us Christians" (*Apology* II, 13). This is not an attitude indicating arrogance, but gratitude—gratitude for all the truth of God and his creation: the truths of science, art, sociology and psychology, as well as the truth of faith. Throughout Christian history great thinkers have pointed to the fact that all knowledge is the province of the believer, that we have nothing to fear and everything to gain from the pursuit of truth wherever it may be found. We must, as Augustine writes, mine the riches out of the secular culture:

> All branches of human learning have not only false and superstitious fancies . . .
> but they contain also liberal instruction which is better adapted to the use of
> truth, and some most excellent precepts of morality; and some truths in regard
> even to the worship of the one God are found among them. Now these are, so
> to speak, their gold and silver, which they did not create themselves, but dug
> out of the mines of God's providence. (*On Christian Doctrine*)

John Calvin manifested a similar attitude in *Institutes of the Christian Religion:*

> Whenever, therefore, we meet with heathen writers, let us learn from that
> light of truth which is admirably displayed in their works, that the human
> mind, fallen as it is, and corrupted from its integrity, is yet invested and
> adorned by God with excellent talents. If we believe that the Spirit of God is
> the only fountain of truth, we shall neither reject nor despise the truth itself,
> wherever it shall appear, unless we wish to insult the Spirit of God.

Further, not only must we rejoice in what we can learn from secular sources,
but we should not belittle the importance of making ourselves knowledge-
able in fields other than that of faith and theology. We must work to bring
God's redemptive work to bear on every area of knowledge. As Francis
Schaeffer wrote in "Two Contents, Two Realities":

> We must consciously reject the Platonic element which has been added to
> Christianity. God made the whole man; the whole man is redeemed in Christ.
> And after we are Christians, the Lordship of Christ covers the whole man.
> That includes his so-called spiritual things and his intellectual, creative and
> cultural things; it includes his law, his sociology, and psychology; it includes
> every single part and portion of a man and his being.

Can we learn the humility to avoid the attitude that as Christians we have a
corner on the truth? Instead, let us be open to learning even from those with
whom we violently disagree. This is more than charity and courtesy; it is wisdom.

Learning from Nonbelievers

As the Israelites came up out of bondage in Egypt, so the Christian must
rise out of the limitations of the modern secular worldview. We have, as they
did, found the promise of freedom. In our case, we can be free from the stifling effects of a view of the world that ignores the basic truths of God's

existence, power and love, and our human sinfulness and self-deception. To grasp these truths radically changes the way we think and live. But the Israelites did not leave Egypt without "plundering" their captors. They brought with them whatever they could that was valuable, useful and worthy. So, too, we must not neglect to make use of the truths we can find in so-called secular thought. Of course, there is no such thing as secular truth as opposed to Christian truth. There are only true and false ways of thinking. The true ways of thinking are those rooted in correct interpretations of one or both of God's two forms of revelation. We must see that we can learn much from our "Egyptian" captors!

Christian values and ideas have influenced our culture so deeply that even unbelievers hold to remnants of truth. That is one of the reasons why we stand to learn much from non-Christians. Perhaps this situation is in the process of changing. The Christian worldview is less and less acceptable to many moderns; hence, the common ground is shrinking. However, despite increasing secularization, it is still true that most of our moral foundations, institutions and attitudes are ultimately based on Christian principles. The last couple of centuries may have distorted these principles, but the Christian influence in our culture is far from extinguished.

One reason we can learn from unbelievers is that Christianity is about *truth* and *reality.* Believers and unbelievers alike share the same reality. When authors write about the human condition, they cannot escape the deep truths about human nature and humankind's sinfulness. Many great novelists and philosophers, for example, have written about humanity's fallenness without ever using that phraseology.

To be able to show the connection between the gospel and human need, we must take the time to truly understand those whose worldview is different than ours. Many people give patently false answers to the basic human questions. To counteract their misleading teachings, we must clearly hear what they are saying and bring the instruments of Scripture and human reason to bear on these issues. Thus we need to be aware of their ideas as well as biblical teachings.

When we as believers become arrogant, thinking that we have a corner on the truth, let us remember that God used the Assyrians as a tool to correct Israel. These idol worshipers were God's instrument to shape his people. When we are open enough today, he uses modern thinkers to correct the church. Though most of us would have serious disagreements with the likes of Marx, Sartre and Nietzsche, they have some powerful words of correction that the church would do well to hear: words about authenticity, pharisaical attitudes, justice and our current ineffectuality. Gregory, an early church father, suggests that we use secular culture as the Israelites did when they went to the Philistines to have their knives sharpened: we must learn to read dialectically, engaging in a conversation with the author, questioning, challenging, as well as learning.

We have a phrase in English, "giving the devil his due," which seems to have originated in Shakespeare's *Henry IV*, Part One. *The Oxford English Dictionary* defines the meaning of this phrase as "to do justice even to a person of admittedly bad character or repute (or one disliked by the speaker)." We need humility, fairness and objectivity to admit the truth, from whatever source it may come.

One final important point must be made. In order to navigate through the complexity and confusion of modern thought, we must have a thorough understanding of the Christian worldview. We must be intimately acquainted with the Scriptures if we are to discern the false teaching that may come along with the good insights. We can use the Bible as a plumb line against which modern deviations are measured and thereby avoided. Obviously this is a hard and demanding call: to know the riches of Scripture and our Christian tradition while, at the same time, taking the time to know and understand our culture and its ideas. But it is a call to truly Christian thinking.

If we can capture this vision, we can make a mark on our culture for Christ by bringing our perspectives to the table in any discussion with humility, creativity and boldness. Let us open our minds to read widely and wisely. This discerning openness is a force that can not only transform each of us but also transform our world.

Name Index

Title Index